TIME
FOR
A
CHANGE

TIME
FOR
A
CHANGE

Richard A Bandler

Meta Publications Inc.
P. 0. Box 1910, Capitola, CA 95010
(408) 464-0254 Fax (408) 464-0517

Library of Congress Card Number 93-084505
I.S.B.N. 0-916990-28-1

Table of Contents

Induction

This book, and all the books related to it, grew out of a goal. We all know of stunningly accomplished people. We usually call them creative. Some of them, even geniuses, had less training, intelligence, talent, strength, energy, money, memory, you name it, than many mediocre achievers in the same field. Why?

Call it a fluke. Rude, but it gets us off the hook. Unfortunately, it sounds less convincing every time. Worse, creative people have an alarming tendency to stay increasingly creative. This flagrant violation of entropy and justice admits no previous explanation.

Two decades ago, the founders of neuro-linguistic programming (NLP) sought to answer that "why" usefully. With a functional answer to that question, we could train people to perform like geniuses.

Today, thousands of people have certifications in NLP. In single sessions, they can accelerate learning, neutralize phobias, enhance creativity, improve relationships, eliminate allergies, and lead firewalks without roasting toes. NLP achieves the goal of its inception. We have ways to do what only a genius could have done a decade ago.

In this book you will find more powerful ways to understand, shape, and use your states of consciousness, your driving beliefs, and your experience of time itself. You can apply these to accelerate learning, achieve your ideals, contribute to others, and have a spectacularly good time. Start now. You already have.

You can read for the fun alone. The text came from a very entertaining workshop. You may later enjoy acting out the workshop in your mind. Do that well and you will save yourself money, trouble, and especially time.

You can go further. When I first met Richard Bandler, people said he demonstrated what he talked about while he described it. That became a cliché. Now he demonstrates a lot more than he describes.

As a result, you can learn even more from this book than what it is about. The original audience heard it once. You can read it twice. On a third reading, you may wish to study the nature of the text.

A misplaced word might have purpose. Two kindred strings of phonemes may appear pages apart, and urge unconscious associations. Anecdotes may elicit representations that prefigure chapters to come. Non sequiturs, senseless digressions, and irrelevant references may serve to chain states or access resources, to aim and amplify the results of an exercise. Grammatical awkwardness may contain a hidden message. Absolutely concise logical paragraphs simultaneously convey other meanings. Often demonstration subjects have done the demonstration and gained the results before approaching the stage.

So much for the first chapter. The reader who concentrates on these details could miss the house for the doorknobs. Enough.

Analysis may entertain. Application rewards.

People who use these understandings have a pair of common complaints. They run into a wall, or they run out of things to do. You might find old beliefs that seem especially hard to change, and new beliefs that seem especially hard to start—or run out of old beliefs to change and new beliefs to install.

Sometimes a belief may seem resistant. You may want to leave it as is. You can get back to it later. You might have other changes to make first.

If you run out of beliefs, you may enjoy reading for presuppositions. Find presuppositions that would do you good to believe. Give yourself those beliefs. You can do that with any book. Presuppositions from the papers of M.H. Erickson have proven valuable to me.

Who are the most valuable people you know of? What led them through their wisest decisions? What beliefs would you like to share with them?

I would like to dedicate this work to a few of the geniuses of our time:

Moshe Feldenkrais, Patrick Moraz, and Anthony Robbins.

— R.B.

Prologue

Before teaching, before learning, before knowing, begin with something more. Teaching and learning and knowing must mean more than recapitulation. To teach, install good learning strategies. To make that worth having, do more. You can install in people something much stronger. Call it hope.

Build powerful hope for people. Build it not so much from understandings. Build hope from an experience. Create this experience. Reality is built from ideas. Create this experience repeatedly. Most of the time, most people have that backwards.

At one time there were no aircraft. At one time there were no automobiles. At one time there were no combs. At one time there was no money, no language. Only by ideas did these things appear in reality.

Share reality. People often, with NLP, changed personal history too much. That rapidly became worse than worthless. I call that learning schizophrenia. Schizophrenics get lousy rooms, bad food, and no zippers. Through shared reality, things have value.

You can not only build ideas, and build reality from them, you can do so ecologically and methodically. That applies to hypnotic techniques, or NLP techniques. It applies to any technique that has to do with ideas.

Take mathematical equations. People can build equations that have no value. The object is to build the equations so that the bridge does not fall down, especially when cars go across it.

Many bridges didn't work. The assumption "Something is wrong," doesn't even work well in medicine. Yet they still try to build from it. That includes practically everything from medicine.

In psychology they still try to build from the model called normative statistics. That allows you to say, "This works sometimes and not others." It does not allow you to describe how this works, or what the work is based on. You want other materials, and other models, even just to design technique.

Design hope. It pays off. People create ideas that will shape reality. Those ideas can become reality to share.

Maybe you want to believe that you're the only person who's competent. Everybody else thinks you're not. You can convince yourself. That will make you convincing to them. Then you can do surgery, or NLP, or drive a bus. They might let you. With luck, they stop you before a terminal adventure.

Go to London. They tell you the right side of the road is the wrong side of the road. People argue philosophically. But in London, or in America, you drive on the side of the road everyone has agreed to—or you collide.

You want to become competent at whatever you do. That does not mean to get phobics, who shake in their boots while their blood pressure blows through the roof, to believe, "This is not fear." The object is to get them to stay calm and alert, and to stay in their own lane, and to drive across the bridge, which remains standing.

Ask yourself, "Can we build better?" To build those things we have to be able to suspend whatever belief system we already have. Keep it out of the way.

Make a distinction between these beliefs and, for example, religious convictions. We're not talking about religion, or beliefs about God. Those things get very, very personal.

We're talking about basic beliefs regarding human capability. Here's the only truth about that. Nobody knows.

It fascinates me that when you cut your finger it heals. How? Also, it knows when it's done. You don't grow a Siamese twin. Something has to tell those cells "Stop." It does not use a higher brain function. Doctors and biologists have no idea how healing even stops.

Science doesn't know everything. Wow. My guess is science doesn't suspect anything. They don't take into account acupuncture. They don't take into account traditional medicine of China or of India or of anywhere. If they can't see it, and they don't know it, and they can't explain it, they say, "When you show me how it works then I'll believe it." Yet they believe in the most idiotic things, that they can't show nobody nothing of.

We don't know how electricity works; we don't know how magnets work. One thing I can guarantee you. Psychologists do not know how people work.

Take somebody who's schizophrenic, or the most highly educated and touted physicist in the world, or somebody who thinks they're the best neurolinguistic programmer. What they can't do is based on what they don't know.

Only in one field did people even briefly get away with saying "We know everything." That was optics. For a while after explaining rainbows most opticians said, "Yes, we've learned everything. We know everything to know about our field." That was so wrong it was ridiculous. Somebody invented lenses that aren't based on two-dimensional space. Suddenly people who scarcely had sight at all could see, walk around, and shave. They just couldn't read. Lasers and light fibers, and who knows what else, kept happening.

Now they know they don't know. Enough happened. It still does. Plan on it.

You can be sure we don't know. We can't know ultimate truth. We can build and assume more functional beliefs.

We can build beliefs, especially with hypnosis. Many people believe they can't go into a trance. They don't even know what it is yet; in fact, they're carrying out a post-hypnotic suggestion. Some experience made them believe they can't.

We have beliefs that our parents give us, that therapists give us, that defeatists give us, or that popped up when we slipped on a banana peel. We can go into a trance and build a suggestion. There is no necessary difference between those.

Start out with saying, with knowing, "You will do this easily and quickly." Have every cell of your neurology agree with it. You've got to believe. With that, you give it your full-tilt boogie.

Without belief you wind up doing the dance with part of you, and not with the other part of you. You can't do congruence. If you don't develop congruence, you have to do therapy for the rest of your life. That's your punishment. Either that, or you have to become a college professor and discuss it for the rest of your life.

The technology presented here only make transformation expeditious. It is not true yet. It probably will be at some time, because it has been so functional for so many people.

Many "not hypnotizable people" have come to me. By having them make it so that they believe that they can, suddenly they can do all these things. In part, that's because they do actually do them. In technical terms, they stop screwing around. They go for it.

Create experiences worth sharing.

—Richard Bandler with Janus Daniels

I

Believer Modification
Install the NLP Attitude

First study great communicators and great clients. I did. That revealed a basic fault in the whole foundation of psychology. So I built something else.

When psychologists studied phobias, they went out and found hundreds of people with phobias. They went after the only people who did not know how to get over the problem! I took another approach. I went out and found two people who had a phobia and who got over it. Then I found out what they did.

I learned this from Milton Erickson, who had unique talents. When his clients had a problem, he always looked at who didn't have it. He then found a way of making the ones who had the difficulty like the ones who didn't.

I saw him work one time with a nut. No two ways about it. This lady could not tell real from not real. She walked in with her psychiatrist. He gave his long exotic psychiatric description about what was wrong with her. You could sum it up by saying, "She's nuts."

She was nuts in a specific way. Basically, this woman could not tell the difference between something that really happened and something that she made up or that somebody described to her.

That's a nice thing about nuts. They are never nuts randomly. They are always nuts this way or that way. It's systematic.

Her psychiatrist flew with her down to Arizona to meet Milton. After the psychiatrist gave his description, Milton turned and said to this lady, "And you left your house and drove here in a green station wagon and saw the countryside on the way, and how long did it take you to get here?" She said, "Twenty-six hours." In fact, they flew there in an airplane and it took two hours. She had no way of sorting those things apart.

Milton, above and beyond putting her into a very, very altered state, used that altered state to build the skill she needed. He knew that she was not functioning. He also knew the exotic reason why. She didn't know how!

I like where Milton got his information. He turned around, looked at the psychiatrist and pointed to the trance chair. This man had all his degrees. He even ran the Erickson Institute in one state. He suddenly displayed what I call deep and over-whelming fear. He looked at the client like this, and Milton said, "Now, just to reassure the lady, I'd like you to show her that trance is not dangerous."

Immediately my brain said, "It must be dangerous! Especially for him! Right now!" He walked over and just as he began to sit, just as he reached the point of no return in sitting, Milton said, "All the way into a trance." As the guy dropped he went, "Klunk!"

Milton said, "Now, as you sit there, I want you to review in your mind three things that you know absolutely and totally happened. Think about events that you're absolutely sure of, not profound events, but, 'Did you have breakfast this morning?'" Milton took him through three events which had occurred that day, and then said, "In your mind go and make up three events." Milton then told him to go into an even deeper trance, and his unconscious mind would convey to him how he knew which ones were which.

Now, I was sitting there at the time, drifting in and out of trance. Everyone always did around Milton. The difference was that I grew up in the '60s. I'd got used to being stoned. So I stopped. I got one thing from what this gentleman said. The pictures looked different. About the pictures of what really happened, Milton asked, "What's the difference?" The therapist literally said, "They seem square, whereas the other ones are vague and transparent and don't have a shape."

By this time the client had also dropped into a trance. Milton said, "Fortunately and conveniently the client has already entered an altered state." Meaning, he'd zoned her through the floor.

He turned around and began to instruct her to review the events then occurring. He told her to put them into square pictures. Then he made up fantasies and told her to make them vague and transparent and without any shape. He began to instruct her unconscious mind to start to sort out all events this way. Nowadays, TVs being mostly square, I recommend you make sure you have other ways to sort real from not real.

This became one origin of something that I developed, along with my friends Chris Hall and Todd Epstein and other people who help me; something we now call submodalities. You can call submodalities the currency of the mind. We can exchange and make change with them.

Objections to Objectivity

People have talked about subjectivity and objectivity for a long time.

When I went to college I didn't get into psychology. For one thing, the research people and the clinicians wouldn't talk to each other. It seemed to me that if, in medicine, the researchers didn't like the practitioners and didn't tell them what they had developed, and the practitioners wouldn't ask for what they needed, then they would kill us.

The research people thought themselves very prestigious. They tortured rats. The practitioners were outside feeling up trees and trying to get in touch with themselves. The field went off into the ozone, which started disappearing, as did those psychologists, because they went overboard.

I had professors who talked about objective experiments. I had a background in physics. Physicists knew that objectivity had long been out of the question. Through Einstein we had learned that things are not objective. They are relative. They depend upon your point of view.

Einstein talked about riding on a beam of light. Pretend you could ride on a particle of light, a photon. Another person charged along on another photon. How does that look different from sitting on a bridge, watching people go by on photons? What if two people, riding two photons together, throw a handball from one to the other? From the perspective of the photon riders, it would look like the ball went straight across. From the bridge, as they passed by, the ball would look like it moved at an angle. On top of all that, time and space work differently for lightspeed.

The idea that things might be relative in psychology took me to objective subjectivity. While I investigated things, people continued to talk about subjectivity as a sin. Now, I happen to like sin. I wanted to know how it works.

This is true of our whole field. In things we look at, from hypnosis to physics to whatever, we seek the subjective experience. In modeling, we explore the subjective experience of the experts. How do they do it? We take that so we can influence people in the same way. Better than thinking of things as good or bad, we want to know about function: "How do you do it?"

We'll do a few bits like cooking from a cookbook. There isn't a good or bad chocolate cake, until you bite in. From a recipe you learn a basic structure by which to do things. After that everybody makes little changes to their own tastes.

In the next few days, I want to give you the foundation of what I got from Milton, and some of the other greats. More, you can begin to give yourself the foundation. Then you can take whatever you do with beliefs or hypnosis and make it more profound.

The Trick Belief

A most enlightening thing happened to me after I got back from seeing Milton. I hypnotized anything that moved in those days. I wanted to find out whether what he said worked. I didn't care about scholastic truth. I did want to know what you could do if you went full-tilt boogie and tried everything.

So I bought the book *Advanced Techniques of Hypnosis and Therapy*. It includes years of Erickson's journal articles. It describes different states he induced and many different hypnotic effects like time distortion, color blindness, limited hearing, you name it.

At the time we had an experimental group—grad students, the guinea pigs of humanity! For nine months, once a week, we got together and tried everything. If we couldn't do it, we did it differently.

Hypnotic lore had acquired the notion called susceptibility. Hildegard at Stanford "proved" that some people could be hypnotized and some couldn't. He left out, however, what we in linguistics call the performative. That means who or what actually performs, actually does the work. So we asked, "Hypnotized by whom?"

We took people and experimented with them. Some people could easily do everything. Some people could do everything after learning how. A few people could go into a deep trance but could do nothing.

One day I was sitting at a table with a friend and the picture for the cover of *The Structure of Magic*. He went into a deep trance. His eyes closed. I said that when he opened his eyes the picture would be gone. I then told him to go inside and count to ten. At the count of ten, the picture would be gone.

This guy had become discouraged. He'd gone through six months of total hypnotic phenomena failure. As he started to count, I picked up the picture. I slid it under the table. He opened his eyes and went, "Uuuuuahhhh!" I instantly said, "That's right! Now close your eyes." I put the picture back on the table.

When he opened his eyes he said, "God!" I said, "You know, this means that you can do anything." From that day forward, he could do any hypnotic phenomenon: any hallucination, time distortion, anything. I won't even tell you what he could do outside hypnosis.

I built a belief in him, however primitively. Nothing had changed in the outside world. Nothing had changed in his neurological structure. Only belief had changed.

Belief in Hypnosis

That got me to ask, "How do beliefs work?" For hypnosis, as for many things, beliefs make the express train taking people far into altered states quickly and effectively. Improve the beliefs people have about their abilities, not just in trance, but in the world at large. Use the fast train.

Many people think that when you go into a trance you lose control of yourself. In fact, you gain control. You gain the ability to control your heart rate, your blood pressure, your ability to remember, your ability to use physical strength or dexterity, your ability to control time and your perceptions. You'll start doing those kinds of things by the end of this. That will increase the range of your abilities with yourself and with other people. Learn both sides, and both responsibilities. Then you can know what control means, and what it's good for.

We work with very simple building blocks. How many of you have experience with submodalities? Actually you've all used submodalities your whole life without knowing it.

Attitude Par Excellence

Notice differences between the way others teach and the way I teach. Grant some importance to your attitude. NLP means more than a methodology. It also means the attitude you have when using it. If you don't have powerful beliefs that you can do anything...

Stop right now. Take a few minutes to learn something. Close your eyes. Think of your personal problem persons. Think of those who, when one walks in, a little voice in your head says, "Oh shit!" Just close your eyes and go back to that. Look at them. Choose one person. As you see that person walk in, hear precisely where that little voice comes from and notice how it makes you feel. If you make that picture bigger and brighter, you'll probably feel worse. Right?

Now try a different way. I recommend that people try this before working with clients. Regardless, pretend your person is a client of yours.

Picture a ravine with a mountain on either side. Blow it up till it fills a forty by forty foot screen. Down at the end of the ravine, I'd like you to put your client. Make them very small. You can put a touch of lightning on top of each mountain.

Just in front of you, put a forty foot puma—one roaring big cat. Swell up in your mind as you step into the scene and inside that cat. From the viewpoint of that cat, look at your client hungrily. As you continue looking down at the person, paw the ground once and see it shake. See the fear in your client's eyes. You can now hear thunder rumbling very loudly, and you can roar louder.

Now take this picture and make it bigger and bigger. Make the colors bright. You can now hear yourself say, as you look down at your client, "Your ass is mine!" Notice if this makes you feel rather different.

If you don't notice any change, check your pulse. Find out if you have one. Because as you blow that picture up, you can also turn up the volume. Now put two hundred black singers on either mountain singing, "Go for it! Change their ass!"

Belief Building Blocks

Take your attitude and begin to really believe that it is your job to do something for people. You don't just let them grow. They came. They paid you to change their lives. By God you're going to do it.

Call this attitude building. Now, if you go in with that attitude, you need only to add generous amounts of skill. We make skills out of the same kinds of building blocks. Take that movie.

As you take that picture I want you to make it bigger. I want you to turn up the volume for the singers louder and louder. Make it surround sound. Bring that image up closer. How does that make you feel? Does it change the intensity of your feelings? If so, keep turning it up until it gives you more and more internal personal power. Instead of saying, "Oh, shit," when you look down at your client, you begin to say to yourself, "Piece of cake!"

You did the same thing when you started to walk. You took very small pieces, one step at a time, and put them together into a foundation to explore a whole new world of activity; a world of learning, a world of understanding, a world of more control in your own environment.

Reorient yourself for a moment. Ask yourself some questions. Examine your own mind for a minute.

You could trick a client. To take the picture off and put it underneath won't work with every client. That guy, at that time, in that place, never expected it. That trick changed his belief. The important part was not moving the picture. The important part was changing his belief.

Placebo Power

You may have thought that a placebo works because the person doesn't know it's a placebo. It works because of belief. In the United States we do an unusual thing. We test all drugs against placebos. That's what a double blind test does. So we have more information on placebos than we have on all drugs put together.

Robert Dilts and I had an idea. We decided to put out a product, tiny empty capsules, called "placebo." No side effects.

Robert was my grad student at the time. He reviewed the research on standard problems like headaches. We made plans to publish a little booklet with an index. A person would look up headaches and read, "When tested against other drugs, placebos work five out of six times." Then it would say, "Take seven when you have a headache." It's a sure thing.

The FDA complained. They told us the effects would wear off. Placebo would loose its efficacy. We knew that could happen. Some people would not get the beliefs built in tenaciously the first time. We revealed our back up plan. "NEW! PLACEBO PLUS! TWICE THE INERT INGREDIENTS! TWICE AS POWERFUL AS EVER BEFORE!"

Of course, drug companies run the FDA. So they wouldn't let us do it. They couldn't find any danger. The capsules were empty. There was nothing there. They told us this was illegal and immoral. "Besides," they said, "it will never work, so we won't let you do it."

We had proved that it would work. We had decades of their experimental results from them. We also had our own results.

My clients often knew a placebo when they got one. They still do. I actually give them the ability to believe that it works because it is a placebo. I explain that since they already know it for a placebo, it will work forever. It does. The structure of how a belief works is where I want you to start.

Unhypnotizability

You can learn a lot about tempo and tonality. You can practice with tape recorders, CD players, metronomes and more. We have much more elaborate equipment than you actually need.

More than one book says *"tempo and tonality have no effect when doing deep trance work."* Pretend you can hear that said by Mickey

Mouse and Muhammad Ali. I think they have some impact. You can realize that tempo and tonality didn't have any effect because the guy who wrote that couldn't affect his tone or tempo.

Non-believers did an experiment in the days when they really tried to make me look like a fraud. I conducted a seminar with three hundred and fifty people. Two psychiatrists from Hildegard's lab brought up a little lady. They said, "This lady is a documented Hildegard zero. She cannot be hypnotized." The shrinks, on either side of the lady, held her up.

She had a spaced-out look on her face. I know a trance when I see one. They repeated, "She can't be hypnotized." She began nodding her head.

I thought we could do a little demonstration. I took her around back and brought her up to a barstool on the stage. I swiveled it around and put her in it with her back to the audience. I told her to relax for a minute.

Then I went around and announced to the audience that these two nice people from Hildegard's place at Stanford had brought us this unhypnotizable person. I wanted to show them that in fact some people could not be hypnotized. I still wonder how any people can be hypnotized by a monotone second rate induction from a tape recorder, which is what Hildegard did. I chose not to mention that.

Then I turned the stool around and told her, "If I said, 'Close your eyes now!' you wouldn't be able to." And she went close-eyed, *cluugghhh*. Why? Because there's a distinction between sitting on a chair, listening to a tape recorder, in a lab room—and sitting on a barstool, listening to a real person while looking out at three hundred and fifty faces. That makes a perceptual difference.

Shouldn't we all have an audience of hundreds of people in our offices? Trance work would get much easier. This woman had never been in front of an audience of that size. She looked out at that sea of faces. It altered her state of consciousness. So as she gasped, and I said, "Close your eyes!" she went inside like a slingshot.

Subsequently, she achieved almost every deep-trance phenomenon. I demonstrated them as things she couldn't do. I stood a little bit in front of her and said, "If I were to lift up her arm like this it should just stay there." I let go. It did. But I didn't look back at her. People kept going *"Uuuggghhh!"* and pointing to get my attention. It's always nice to preserve that. They pay closer attention.

Exploring Beliefs

I want you to start something very simple. Go inside and think of something that you *categorically* believe. Pick something free from emotional meaning. I know that some of you have a background in psychology. Cure yourself of that! Trust me. Think of something like, "Do you believe the sun is going to come up tomorrow?" Don't pick, "Do you believe you're a person of worth?" Make it simple so it works. As soon as you start attaching meaning it gets less effective. Emotion up; information down.

Did you draw stick figures on a pad of paper when you were kids and then flip through them? It creates the effect of the stick figure moving. Have you seen that kind of thing? If I drew one of those pads but only gave you one picture a week for five years, how much of a pattern would your mind make out of it? You wouldn't see what was going on. Yet if you just flip through it once... That's how the brain works. It learns by doing things quickly and simply. It makes patterns.

Fast Philia

It's easier to cure a phobia in ten minutes than in five years. I pulled that trick for ten years before I knew enough to tell anybody. I didn't realize that the speed with which you do things makes them last.

I was able to cure a phobia. Other people weren't. Some people used the same technique and still couldn't.

I taught people the phobia cure. They'd do part of it one week, part of it the next week and part of it the week after. Then they'd come to me and say, "It doesn't work!" If, however, you do it in five minutes, and repeat it till it happens very fast, the brain understands. That's part of how the brain learns.

I had more impatience that they. They sat around wanting to drag it out for an hour. I wanted people in and out in five minutes so I could get on my way. That paid off for my clients.

I discovered that the human mind does not learn slowly. It learns quickly. I didn't know that. I just move quickly.

Everything else in the universe seems to work that way. If you take sheet metal and bend it quick and hard, it will hold its shape. If you bend it quick and hard enough, it can break. If you just slowly push it, it'll bend right back. To make things stay, use speed.

If you want ideas to take shape, the same principle applies. Suppose you run somebody through the fast phobia cure. In order for that to work people need to go through the steps quickly, especially when they rewind it at the end. The speed with which they do it makes it hold. I don't use it anymore. For me, it's too slow.

For pacing sometimes I grab hold of you. Either keep up or skid. You can pace till you get into people's shoes. Do that for empathy. Do empathy with happily married Nobel Prizewinners who party well and wisely. Pace victims to know how to get them to respond. Then inch them out of whatever they got stuck in. Pace to lead.

Slow Learning

You have the option of making the Montessori mistake, the ultimate pace. Teach kinesthetic kids kinesthetically, always. Visual kids, pace them in visual language, forever. That leads to crippling them their whole life! Get people to use everything they can as fast as they can.

Babies start learning to speak. They don't even know that language exists. Children can learn language quickly. They can learn foreign languages while barely knowing their native language. Our school system utterly fails to teach it. We do it for twelve years so that later they can't speak a word of it.

Another problem is where we teach language. When I went to school, we sat at a peg board with a set of headphones. Every utterance in the language became associated with a peg board. I took Spanish. I went to Mexico. I heard Spanish. I saw the peg board. I relived being in school. It didn't help me communicate. But it was fun, if you like peg boards.

Throw somebody in Mexico. Give them two bottles of tequila. They speak lingua franca by morning. Do more than joke about these things. Take them to heart. This is your life. It's our children's lives.

As soon as I stopped thinking about it, I just went out and had fun and did things with people and related to people. Then you learn the language. That applies to everything. But people don't use it.

The Possibility Problem

People think of what they can't do. I have done generative seminars. I've said, "This is not for remedial change, come in because you want good things." People come. They don't come in and allow the scope to even conceive of the possibilities.

They come in and say, "I want to get rid of my internal dialogue." I say, "Kill yourself, you won't have any." They say, "Wait a minute…"

They need to understand, to dream of what's possible. They don't even know the problem. They first took the step of thinking, "I know the solution! If I didn't have internal dialogue then I'd feel good. Then I'd be enlightened." Instead they could realize that we can choose what to make a problem and decide what process we use.

They could talk inside themselves like Mozart. They'd have an opera motivating them. Then they'd want to keep all their voices. They'd have a great laugh like Mozart. Their world would resonate with music and excitement instead of nasty voices whining and screeching.

Decisive Details

Whatever gets in the way, move through quickly, so that they can't keep up with it. Move that fast. The faster we drive, the less detail we can pay attention to. People get caught in details. We don't know when to go fast and when to go slow. That causes bad decisions.

The value of detail depends on what you want to learn. We learn to drive across a bridge. Do you want to inch your way across? Have all the possibilities of falling inch across your mind? You want to have an outcome, to get there. Add a way to enjoy the process.

People in the military learn to walk across a board. They walk across a board an inch off the floor. Put it up 20 feet. They move slower than they do on the ground. They look at the ground, taking in data they don't need. They only need data about the board. If they did it the same way that they did on the ground, they could have the same result. By being over aware of height, they become over aware of the possibility of falling.

Sometimes information is relevant, sometimes not. Build a belief that says, "Look at the board and go across. There's no difference." Filter and select the information to keep track of.

In Houston, I climbed as high as what we had, tall trees, maybe a ledge. With everything flat, up seems a lot more up. I remember the first time I saw guys working on a skyscraper. I looked up there. They just trucked around on those beams. I thought, "These guys have gone out of their minds."

But I was 17 stories up, looking up at them, thinking this, as if another 17 really made a difference. Suddenly I looked down. How far do you really have to fall to splat? Above a certain height we really don't make anything else.

They want to keep track of things. They keep track of things like tools and wind. That one thing I did learn to keep track of. I was standing on a platform. Even though I had a floor, the wind almost blew me off. I was busy looking up at them. I didn't watch where to go. They saw it coming. Before it ever arrived, they leaned into it. They had the senses to reach out and notice it. The gust caught me.

Build beliefs that tell you, "Design your perceptions, and design your behaviors, around the task. Then the task becomes simple." If you don't, then you get the opposite effect. You get too much education.

Deconstructing Beliefs

Now I want you to stop and think of something that you absolutely, utterly and totally believe. Just stop. Think about it. Think of something you know.

I want you to pay attention to the following distinctions. Notice what happens when you're asked, "Is the sun coming up tomorrow?" Notice how you represent an emphatic. The sun will rise.

I know you probably studied existentialism in college. You can argue about anything anyway. But the question is, "Do you believe it or not?" To find out "Can you philosophize about it?" go back to college. If you must, pick something like, "Is breathing useful?"

When you choose one, I want you to notice things about it. Does the voice come from this side or that side? Does it come from your head, in front of you, behind you? Does it move? Does it go up and down? To the side? All the way around? Some voices come from the back, some from the front.

Have you read anything by Stephen King? How would you like to have his internal dialogue? Not me! For part of his motivation strategy he has a voice maybe two feet behind him that sounds like it comes from a deep subway. It roars, "Get to work!" This will keep you motivated.

Also pick something that could be true or not true. It's not that it's not true, it's just a maybe. Take the game next week. "Aaahh. Could be this, could be that." Or, "What do you want for lunch?" You might say, "Aaaahh, I don't even know if I'm going to eat lunch." Pick something that may or may not be true.

Go through this with me a little bit at a time. Take both, one at a time. First think about what you believe. Then think about what may or may not be the case. Now you have a belief and a doubt.

I especially want you to notice *where* the pictures are. Are your images in a different location? Is one up and the other down? Is one to the right and the other to the left? Are they in the same place?

Belief and Doubt

You sir. Look at one. Now look at the other. Notice if they're in different places. Are they? Yes, the strong belief is straight ahead and lower; the doubt is to the left. How about the rest of you? You will find something different for everybody.

These are such stuff as subjectivity is made of. You've all got pictures, voices, feelings, music, taste, balance, smell. That's what there is.

About subjectivity you can't be wrong. It's the one thing in life that you *can't be wrong* about. It's *your own* subjectivity. If a picture looks like it's on the right, that's where it looks like it is.

Go through your representations. Look at one, then look at the other. Is one picture bigger? Is one brighter? Is one closer? Is one in color and the other in black and white? Or are they both in color, both in black and white? Is one a slide, like a still snapshot? Or are they both movies? Is one in focus and the other out of focus? Is one three-dimensional and the other two-dimensional?

How about your hearing? Does the voice come from a different direction in one as opposed to the other? Does it have a different tempo? Does it sound like the voice starts closer or further away? Is it your voice or your father's?

Sometimes things break down into something so simple. I once had a client whose representation for something absolutely true was her grandmother's voice. When something wasn't true, it was her mother's voice. She sorted these things out that way. She said she believed she couldn't go into a deep trance. I had her take that belief and change that voice to the other one.

Have you got those distinctions? These are the big chunks. We'll get more details later.

Belief Induction Demonstration

For now, I want you to think about the ability to go into a deeper and more profound trance than you ever thought you could. I want you to do this in a very specific way. Start by putting a picture of yourself in such a trance in the position of something that could or could not be true. Don't put it into the belief position yet. Start out by putting it into the doubt position.

Sir, would you mind helping me for a minute? For you, up and to the left was where something could or could not be. Right? I want you to start by putting the idea that you can go into a deeper trance than you've ever been in right up there. Okay? Now, slowly move it way into the horizon until it hits a point. Then I want you to pull it up quickly, *whhhaccckk!* That quick. Pull it up into the position where a strong and powerful belief is, with the auditory representations you'd have there. Make it the same size, the same closeness, and do it very suddenly. Start now.

That's right… drift all the way down, with a growing sense of comfort and satisfaction and enjoyment about how easy it is to really learn about going into a deep, comfortable and relaxed state. And I want your unconscious to give you real security in the knowledge that you can really learn from your other mind, that you can really learn about making any change and having any skill you want. I want you to know when you want to return to this state, and in fact, to go twice as deep *noowww*. That's right—all the way down.

I want you to see that any time I touch you like this, you can go all the way back, or even if you just feel my hand there you can return. And, of course, if I were to touch you on the other shoulder, you could go back to consciousness and feel absolutely and exquisitely *wonderful*. Now, that's right. All the way back. Are you back here?

"Yeah, pretty back."

Thank you!

II

Believe in Laughter
Frame Problems As Humor and As Something to Enjoy

Now that we have given you the belief that you can go into a more profound trance than you've ever done before, and that you can become highly proficient in doing trance work with clients, it's time to install another ability: *framing things humorously.*

Now, take problems with humor. Humor is a natural function with human beings. People talk about it as a release. In NLP we ask, "Release from what?" Also ask, "How?"

Without humor, you get to do it again. Without laughter, whatever we did, we do. When people feel guilty and moan and groan, they will do the same thing again. We can feel surprised, relieved, and delighted that we notice, and start laughing. Then what happens? We open a door. We can escape that whole world.

People say, "Someday I'll look back and laugh at this." Why wait? It doesn't do you good.

With the ability to laugh, you have the freedom to escape your own model of the world. A lot of times people laugh, but they don't escape. Seize the moment. Use the instant of laughter.

Look at a situation as being as silly as it is. In some other context or some other time it would be. In some other culture it would be. You can change your perceptions enough.

Aliens Too

Imagine what we must look like to aliens. Aliens in movies and TV shows visit earth. They know how to fit in with humans. No way. A pair of aliens down here would get caught right off. Humans are too strange.

Suppose you came here and tried to fit in. Get up with everybody in the morning. Then, we all go in metal machines with wheels and drive really fast in opposite directions beside a painted line.

They think, "This must be one of the weirdest fetishes in this world. They get in these things and drive really fast right next to each other. The ones driving fastest are the one driving in opposite directions right by each other. They could reach out and touch each other. They'd rip their arms off. Frequently they do worse."

To an alien they wouldn't understand, they'd say, "Look, they've learned. In some places they put barriers in between, instead of paint. They build the barriers out of cement. You'd think they'd have the sense to make rubber cars and drive slower so they'd just bounce."

That must look like weird behavior. You could fly at ten times the speed of light. Get right down near the ground and go very fast. That would still scare you. In space you've got nothing to run into.

Then you would notice odd little things like people boiling each other in their backyards. Especially in this town. You figure, "They have to, because they have all these rules for driving that nobody obeys."

So you want to figure out how to fit in. You start to learn our rules to follow them. When are you supposed to and when are you supposed not to? Everybody here knows. We have accepted behavior.

We don't understand any of it. We only do it. We forgot how we started. We don't pay attention anymore.

Those things would seem very, very hard for anybody to imitate. We ourselves can take people who learn to drive in San Francisco and take them to San Diego. Everybody there drives crazy. Take a San Diego driver and put him in San Francisco. Same trouble.

Take any one of them and stick them in London, or Paris, or Rome. It's a whole other world. Some people realize, "That's the way those people drive." Other people go into the fudge factor, "They all have gone nuts."

Now, some days you start thinking that the world went nuts or the world is out to get you. It can happen. Viktor Frankl found things to laugh at and make jokes about as a Jew in Auschwitz.

Anytime you had to feel bad unless other people changed, you had the opportunity to laugh. You still do. Otherwise you have to feel bad for the rest of your life. You don't get to just open up the doorway. Take the aliens' point of view.

Laughter opens doorways. Find a door. Charge through. Claim a new world.

Hypnosis accelerates this. I like that about it. In altered states people do this easily. You build a belief. They go into a powerful altered state. Then take that altered state and install the belief that they can open this doorway, that doorway.

Your family doesn't do what you want. You don't have to freak out. If you do, you don't have to worry about it, and discuss it, for ten years in therapy.

How many people in this world have died because people have figured, "If you don't have the same ideas as me I will kill you." People keep talking, "The problem with guns, the problem with bombs." The problem is that people think agreement is useful, and that matching beliefs has value. "You guys wear diapers on your heads. We light them on fire. If you don't believe in this then we'll kill you."

People do it with themselves on the inside. They build beliefs. They believe they have to be happy. To be happy they believe they have to change something. That means something is wrong. They tell themselves, "Stop internal dialogue." They have some way of doing all this without noticing the silliness, without smiling. Can't they ask, "How do I know I don't feel happy?" At least they only try to kill parts of themselves.

Listen to arguments in operas. What a way to disagree. You can argue in harmony. Alternately, you could develop permanent continuous total everlasting agreement, the monotone mistake. Why do people aspire to monotony?

Realize the reason they don't like their voices inside. They have tooth grinding tonality. They don't get along with other people because their tone of voice sucks.

I've seen somebody, so many times, turn around and yell, "You know I love you!" The tone doesn't match the phrase. You can turn around and sweetly say, "I hate you," with your voice mellifluous enough. They'll smile.

The tone, the expression on your face, all those things communicate forcefully. Words convey little meaning. If we don't get it on the inside of our heads, we'll never get it on the outside. How would you even know?

You can build a pleasant internal state. Trance does that for you. People can laugh at themselves better. People can relax more. Start from a pleasant state. Can you believe we need anyone to tell us these things?

The aliens will find out what we do in our heads. They'll pop out of that fast. Our behavior won't seem so impossibly goofy anymore. Behavior still won't make any sense to rational apprehension. By comparison, however, behavior must remain relatively mundane. The constraint of physical laws limits behavior. What a relief for aliens!

Unaltered Consciousness

Behind a lot of what you see as trance work lies a complementary ability. We talk about altered states of consciousness. That presupposes an ability to maintain something as a normal state of consciousness.

We talk about altering your state and going into a trance. That means to do something different with your consciousness than you normally do. Flexibility in consciousness provides you with all skill.

How many of you here meditate? When you meditate, don't you do something different than you do normally? Isn't that true? You take your consciousness as something that you don't normally do.

When I learned to meditate they gave me a mantra. You say this thing over and over in your head. Not something I did normally. It does alter your state of consciousness. I go into a deep state of utter boredom. It works.

Hypnotic Reality

Milton once went to give a lecture. I loved Milton's description about going up to give this lecture. He had the ability to detect, before his turn, that he had a room full of people who didn't believe in hypnosis. In fact, some of the people had tried to have his license removed. In 1955, they actually tried to take his medical license away for using hypnosis. "He uses something that doesn't exist!"

Think about that—he did something that wasn't there. And it was "bad." Something that wasn't there wasn't good. So they brought him up before a review board. I actually met one of the people on that review board years later. I love his description. It was even better than Milton's. He said, "I remember him, coming in the door? And after that I don't know much of what happened." I thought, "You could sum it up that way."

Milton looked at them and said, "*So you think it's bad for me to put people in a deep trance* and you *can feel it* now it's a bad thing, and I want you to feel comfortable and relaxed in the knowledge that there is no such thing as *going into a trance* too quickly, or too slowly, now. And the knowledge that you learn about going into a trance deeply…that sometimes people are afraid of what's not there. Can you feel that?"

It always amazes me that people will fight over what's not there. People who claim there's no such thing as hypnosis will fight vehemently about it, and go to a hypnosis seminar. The contradictions there! I have people who pay $2500 bucks to go to a hypnosis seminar, and then tell me there's no such thing as hypnosis. Do you pay $2500 bucks for what's not there?

Do they sell subliminal tapes over here? What a scam! What a scam!! They sell you tapes you can't hear! They say, "Listen to this, you can't hear what's on it, so you're not hearing it consciously. Therefore it must be unconscious!" Right!? That sounds like something Tricky Dick or Slick Willy would do.

We had to try this. A friend of mine has a stress clinic. We made a subliminal tape. All the suggestions on it are things like,

"Everything will freak you out. You'll be nervous all day." All you can hear is the sound of the ocean.

We gave it to thirty people. We looked at them and said, "This is the relaxation tape. It has ten thousand suggestions to be more comfortable and relaxed. We want you to listen to it all day, waking up, while you're in the car driving, going to sleep, it will change your life." We know how to say these things.

Notice my spirit of experimentation. You test on other people's lives. They call it "Private Practice."

When these people came back the most amazing thing happened. They categorically said, every one of them, that they had the best, the most relaxed month of their life! So I decided that subliminal tapes were not the answer.

Anyway, Milton got into the situation. He realized he had a room full of skeptics. He told me that he gave, as he said, "an hour and a half lecture in which I delivered no information of any relevance to anything. And I did so, slowly and laboriously, making point upon point that referred to the points that didn't exist before." He said, "It was only the sound of my voice and the tempo at which I spoke that allowed me to know at which moment in time to simply step forward and say, 'You may all close your eyes, *noooww.*' They did."

Milton fought wars about what was legitimate and what was not legitimate. So did Virginia. Virginia actually used to keep it a secret that she did family therapy, or she'd get fired. Even later in her life she hadn't noticed that it was okay. She was having an argument that she had won.

One time, she had just given a lecture trying to convince people that family therapy was legitimate. I pointed out to her, "They are all family therapists!" She said, "Well yes, but they need to know what to say to their bosses." I said, "Most of them are their bosses, Virginia."

The Attitude of Appreciation

Milton Erickson wasn't prone to let his sense of humor out because many people think that if you enjoy something it won't work. Yet if NLP adds anything to the world I hope it's the attitude, "If it ain't fun, it's probably not working." Many of my colleagues have tried to make NLP serious. I've noticed that humor is a powerful tool. Have you noticed that?

When most of us went to school, we had teachers who tried to teach us things while making us feel bad. They did the last part well. So if I write a polynomial on a chalkboard, most people in the room will get sick. When we went to school, they made us sit still in chairs and made us feel bad. They induced fear and anchored it with numbers.

I consider that a poor use of anchoring, but I do it with my own kids. I look at their schoolbooks, induce fear, and anchor it. That's how I can get them to avoid that knowledge. My boy hates his addition book. He cheats: he goes and looks up calculus instead.

When I worked with Milton I observed his way of inducing humor. He did get people to *have a sense of humor*. He would get people to literally *enjoy problems*. He'd get people to be stingy about them.

He had one client I read about in one of his journal articles who dropped by regularly. She had psychotic episodes. Milton had her put them in an envelope and mail it to him. She always described them in the form of a nominalization. So when she had an episode he said, "*Stop!* Just collect it up." She saw little naked men dancing around in the air. So Milton got her to collect them, put them in an envelope and mail them to him. He said, "I will save them for you." Thereafter she would come by now and then to make sure Milton hadn't sold any of them!

I've done the same kind of thing. You can get a client to have pride in what we call disorders. That teaches how to have control over them.

When clients come in I use this formula. I tell them I can't listen to their problems because I'm not a psychologist. "There's a law against mathematicians knowing!" That way I don't have to listen to drivel.

They have to think of me as somebody from a temporary employment agency. I say, "Wouldn't it be nice to have a day off from your problems? Think about it. We all have the same ones constantly. Wouldn't it be nice just to have a day off from your problems? I mean, you get a day off from your job!" Who's going to say no to that? "Just think of me as someone from a temporary agency. If you can describe to me exactly how to have your problem, you get a day off."

I made a film at Marshall University with a woman who had psychotic episodes when people were late. She would fall down, white-knuckled, writhing on the floor. So I asked her, "Okay, how do you do this?" She began to describe *when* to have a psychotic episode. I elicited information from her. To start, she had to make appointments. I said, "Ten minutes after. Do I begin to throw myself on the floor?" And she said, "*No, no, no, no.* You have to edge your way up to it." She taught me.

This kind of attitude Milton had, not only doing therapy, and also inducing deep trance, but in life. I don't know what many of you do for a living, but I teach sales as an application of hypnosis. I've found that hypnotic communication means nothing more than methodically working with consciousness to get results—whether for dentistry, improving your health, or in medicine. Hypnosis involves communicating with words and with experience. More than telling someone about something, induce the states which will make them most effective.

Invest Your Breath Now

Most of you have had some experience with submodalities. I want you to stop and scan your brain. I'm going to have you do a couple of things.

I should point out first that trance work consists of supplying feedback. Part of what it takes to induce a good trance is to pace with your tempo. Primarily, I set up a pace in my tempo with their breathing. This begins before the start of the trance. It begins at least by the time you start talking to them.

At workshops people come up and say, "Oh, it's very nice to meet you." They don't start at the beginning. Then they say, "Now we're going to begin." Life doesn't work that way. In the first five seconds of communication, you want to start pacing people. You can use that to induce whatever you want. You can influence whatever happens, whether it's selling a car, closing a business deal, negotiating, getting a date, whatever. Don't start too late.

Start before the beginning. With all the exercises, as you find your partner, start out doing the exercise. Also, all skills count. If we do one skill and then go on to another, the first one still counts.

It's not like you pace, and then stop. They do that in New York. They think it works.

I want you literally to sit down with your partner. As you begin speaking, gauge the tempo of your speaking on his breathing. Some people's breathing may get hard to see. So try one thing that works. Look at your partner and say, "Take a breath. Now." Then watch where he's breathing. You can see some people breathing low down, some up.

Then begin to take your speech and let it go in the rhythm of his breathing, so that as he breathes in and out, you literally take the tone of your voice up and down. Keep your rhythm and tempo much like what you hear me do, or like what you hear on tapes of any speakers who you really enjoy listening to.

Belief Hypnosis Exercise

Take a piece of paper and elicit the differences between a powerful belief and something that may or may not be true, as I did with this man. Once you've found the differences, have them picture the belief that they can go into a deeper trance than they have ever been in before. "You can go into a trance that will enable you to do things like control your heart rate and blood pressure, do hypnotism, have a better memory, a rich sexual life, etc."

Put that belief in the doubt representation. Then move it out to a point in the distance. Then quickly pull it up into the same submodalities as the strongest belief you can find.

When they think about the sun coming up, they *know* they believe it. They think about going into a trance and doing anything. They know they believe it totally.

If you know anchoring, go ahead and anchor this. When you anchor a strong belief, anchor it one place. When you have them make that shift, fire it off. Go ahead; take about a quarter hour apiece. Remember—you must have fun around me, or I'll hurt you.

Submodalities for Hypnosis Demonstration

I want you to just hold your arm out there like this. That's right. Close your eyes and take a deep breath. What I want you to do is relax and make an image of yourself. See it clearly out in front of you. Now see that image of yourself looking back at yourself relaxing and with a growing sense of anticipation about what you are about to learn.

Now I'm going to give you instructions that are between you and me and *your unconscious*. Because it is your unconscious that is learning. I want you to take that image of yourself and begin to move it away from you. Then move it toward you. If at any point it begins to deepen your trance, I want you to allow your hand to slowly rise up, involuntarily.

Now, slowly begin to move that image away from you. Now, as it moves away from you, I want you to see it get slightly larger, and see if you feel more relaxed as you float down on the waves of relaxation and comfort. Then, very slowly, begin to pull it closer to you, closer and closer. If at any point you feel yourself going deeper, allow your arm to float up; as you feel yourself start to come out of trance allow your arm to float down.

Now begin to make that image bigger and bigger and even bigger still. Again, as you feel yourself *float down* into a trance, deeper and deeper, your hand will go up.

Now I want you to take the image and make it into a movie. I want you to speed up the frames in the movie. In a moment I'm going to be talking to the other people here. And since you know what some of these submodalities are you're going to begin to experiment, to find out what deepens your state, so you can float down, deeper and deeper still, enjoying the sense of relaxation and personal satisfaction and control of your own destiny, as well as your own depth of trance.

Now, how can you begin to find out which changes in which submodalities affect them the most intensely?

For some people, you deepen their internal dialogue to lower and lower tones. For some people, you move the origin of their internal voice further and further away from them. Whether moving the pictures closer or further away, or making the colors brighter, or turning up the brightness of the image itself, it doesn't matter. Find which ones make them feel more and more relaxed, so you can begin to do the following.

Now I'm going to lift up your hand once more. That's right. Just hold it there. I want you to allow this finger to float up, involuntarily, when something deepens your trance. I want you to listen internally to your own voice describing your own internal sense of relaxation. If it deepens your trance, I want you to make that voice get louder and allow your finger to rise up, and if it doesn't I'd like you to allow the finger to go down. That's right. Begin *now*. And then take the voice, and have it move away from you so that it sounds like it's coming from further and further away. That's right—even more. Take your time.

Then take that image of yourself going into a trance and do each of the things one at a time, that made you feel you were going deeper, beginning now, and do them two to three to four times as much. That's right—deeper and deeper still. There you go. All the way down. You can allow your hand to go down, only as you continue to go deeper into a relaxed state, and to enjoy the process of really learning, about the other mind at your own rate, so that each sound and breath, allows you to feel more relaxed, still learning about the other mind, and what *your unconscious* has to teach you. That's right.

We'll increase your sensitivity and skill at a rapid rate. You can begin to develop the tempo and tonality and find out what affects each person. Because with some people, as the images get bigger, they'll go deeper, and as they get smaller...

See, even if you stop right now, think of something you really enjoy doing, something really pleasant. Close your eyes and see what you'd see if you were there; hear what you would hear. Then just turn the volume up and notice if it intensifies your pleasure. Turn the brightness of the image up. Make the image bigger. If this intensifies your pleasure, turn it back the other way and notice if it diminishes. You begin to see that there's a direct link between your own consciousness and your own enjoyment of life.

A lot of times people have things that aggravate them. The more they think of them, the more they get aggravated, the bigger the pictures get. They say, "Perhaps I'm blowing this out of proportion." Have you ever heard anybody say that? Well, they are!

What you want to blow out of proportion is your own enjoyment! What you want to turn down, and turn dark, until you can't see it, is fantasies that interfere with your pleasure in life.

And to do so with a growing sense of comfort. In a minute I'll ask you to take a deep breath and return here, with a very pleasant feeling that will begin right here and just spread, from knowing that you've learned something of value. All the way back—awake, alert. Thank you.

Acuity and Amplifying Responses

Train your eyes. I want you to concentrate on building the ability, the visual perceptions, of noticing which things respond to what.

The other thing is to just have them put their hands out. Make a change in a submodality of this image of themselves going into a trance. If making the picture helps them into the trance, let their hands float up big; if making the picture makes them wake up more, have them lower their hands so that you can visually see.

If you can't see, tell them to do it *more*. People made NLP too hard. When they anchor responses, people train to look for really minimal change. If you can't see it, *make it more dramatic.*

We call this amplifying. Amplify. Turn the dial up to the point where you can tell.

I'll show you how simple this is. I want you to think of that past pleasant experience. Just close your eyes. Now make the picture bigger and bigger. Turn the brightness up even more. Now turn the volume way up. There you go. Fine. Just stop there for a second.

With each of these steps you begin to see more dramatic changes. If the changes aren't dramatic enough, change the submodality even more. Double the size of the image. Double it again. And double it again. Do you notice the changes in her face? This means you don't have to squint to see what goes on.

Sliding Anchors

A lot of you, when you anchor, probably mark a spot. Once you've noticed a change, you can make anchors that I call sliding anchors. When you get the response you want from someone, and then you do something that amplifies it, start at the same place and slide it a little bit further. Then go back to the beginning and *slide* a little bit more... and even more still.

You get a signal that the unconscious understands. You get to the point where you can slide further than you anchored and end up with a more intense response than before. Do you not? Yes you do! Okay, thank you.

Always tell people in trance ahead of time when you're going to touch them. I want you to start out with the anchor you made last time. Go back to your partner and fire off the anchor.

You have to speak one way to the conscious mind and another way to unconscious processes. "I'm going to reach over and reach up your left arm. And I'm not going to tell you to put it down." The unconscious understands that to mean "Hold it there." That means when I tell you to put it down, you will. Call it a presupposition.

Submodalities to Deepen Trance

With his arm up there, inform him that you'll have him make images bigger, and slower and further away, and closer, so that it sounds louder and softer. When any of these things deepen the state of trance, allow his hand to float up so I can see. That means you'll get a more dramatic response. Also tell him to do it with *honest* unconscious movement.

The goal of this leads everything. People must not become conscious to make the decisions. Otherwise they will bring themselves out of trance so they can indicate how they go into trance correctly. That doesn't make any sense. Think about it.

Test the amplifiers to find out which ones really do deepen trance. Out of the submodalities you know, with each person, you'll find three or four amplifiers that will deepen trance more than the others. Not that the others won't, but find the ones that have the most dramatic result.

Then build a sliding anchor. Go through and amplify each of those five and build the same sliding anchor for them. Make sure it works. Now you have a sliding anchor for trance.

Ferocious Frivolity

While you have them in trance I want you to guide them to a time and place where they were quite ferocious and frivolous at the same time. That's the state where you are willing to wantonly *go for it*.

We look for that. Find that state where you go for it, where every fiber of your soul says, "Do this!" I want you to amplify it and anchor that. Then I want you to fire both sliding anchors at the same time and watch them go for a joy ride. Okay? Then bring them out of trance.

Whenever I do trance work with people I want it to be fun. I don't want going into trance something they hold back from. Too many people try to coerce their clients into trance. You can do it. You could take their fears and force them to go into trance against their will, but you wouldn't get good trance results. And we don't get good people from that.

Help people to look at life ferociously and frivolously. Then they see things they want. They go for it. When they see something that needs doing, they do it. That includes going into trance and controlling their neurons and futures. When it's time to make changes, instead of coming back to me dependently, they learn to take what we did. They do it themselves.

Selling Change

Notice the advantages of charging the way I do. I charge by the change and I charge a lot. That builds in motivation to change quickly and independently.

I don't want the basis of what I do to be that somebody gets one change. "Just take the bad things and make them okay." I want people to take the good things and make them *great*.

Most of the people who come to me had a problem that's out of control. They don't realize that what's out of control is that they haven't *focused* on getting to what they want and more. They've often focused instead on getting *away* from what they don't want.

I really want to make a change in individuals. Instead of helping them to move away from something, I want to get them moving towards what feels good, what is good, and what's useful. Working with people that way makes dramatic changes. And that makes your work a lot more fun.

How many doctors in here? People came to you when they got broken, right? What if you got them asking "How can I change my habits, so that I become healthier?" What if they dropped by and paid to find out how to adjust their diets *before* they got sick? What if they wanted to feel as good as they could instead of just coming in and saying, "I hurt, fix me!" That change in mentality makes your work a lot better. Instead of having to see sick people all the time, you see people get less and less sick. Plus, people enjoy seeing you more.

This works for everything. I do great sales training. I teach you to affect people so they *want* to come back—just to see you. Instead of feeling that they got pressured into buying something, they remember they had the time of their lives making a good decision.

To me, salespeople—and all of us to a certain degree—work in the entertainment business. When we forget that, we act too seriously. Then we suffer. That's what makes it *work* instead of fun. The more fun you make your work, the more dynamic you make your work, the better life will be all around. This I guarantee you.

III

Tips From the Lost Manual
"How to Run Your Own Brain"

I wrote *Using Your Brain For a Change* because I thought, "Look, when we get born, our brains should come with an owner's manual." Well, where'd it go? Maybe it gets lost in the placenta.

How many of you have a home computer? Those come with an owner's manual. It usually reads as if they thought you had designed the computer. Read it and you've got about the only way to not know how to use your machine. It doesn't say things like, "Plug it in." I need something that says, "This is the on/off switch. Press it."

They don't tell you, "When you make pictures bigger and brighter, feelings get stronger." So when you think about something that somebody did that hurt you, and you make a big bright picture of it, and it starts to feel bad, you make the picture bigger and you feel worse.

Nor do they tell you, "Stop it!" Everything pretty much boils down to finding out what clients do and telling them to stop it! It might sound funny, but sometimes it boils down to that.

Last year I saw 112 clients between workshops. I would say that with 111 of them I only had to get a detailed account of what they did in their heads, then look at them and ask, "Has it ever occurred to you to just not do this?!" And they said, "Well, no?" They didn't know what they were doing. The 112th one knows who he was. He only needed a good swift kick in the pants to get him to go do anything.

Captivating Therapy

I had one person who was agoraphobic. He never left home. He had never even tried to leave. Call it a wealthy disorder. Agoraphobia is not a pauper's disorder. Suppose you didn't have any money and you had agoraphobia. What would you do for a living? You'd starve. That would be the problem. You've got to have some money to pay rent, have people bringing you groceries, and all that stuff. That makes it a rich people's disorder. I like them. Therapists call and say, "We have an agoraphobic to work with." My wallet goes, "Pulse, pulse, pulse." I'll drop by.

They're easy. I just make it scarier for them to stay home. I just go in and say, "Hi! Nice day for an exorcism, isn't it?! Looks terrible outside. Want to stay here with me and play?"

I love working in a mental hospital. They can't get away. I like the concept. I went to one. The staff told me how impossible the patients were. I thought, "Shit! They haven't seen anything yet."

I don't know how many of you heard the story of Milton with Jesus Christ. Of all the things Milton ever told me, this one didn't work for me. He looked at the guy and said, "I heard you used to be a carpenter." The guy said, "Yeah." Next day, Milton asked, "Do you believe in helping people?"

Then Milton sent him out to work with the guys in the back of the hospital building. They fixed him, not Milton! Take a bunch of redneck guys in Arizona. These guys won't take any shit about you being Jesus Christ. Most of them are Baptists to start with. They'd sharpen their knives and look at your nuts. You'd get un-schizophrenic fast!

But that worked. So when I did some training and some of the residents told me they had this client who believed he was Jesus Christ, who ripped bed sheets off and draped himself in white and all this stuff, I went, "Ouuhhhh!"

I did something simple. I went out and got a carpenter's belt, and one big 4 by 6 and another big 4 by 4 and a whole stack of four-penny nails. Those are suckers about a foot long. And I got a tool belt with a five-pound mallet.

I went in. The guy lay in his bed. I took my tape measure and measured him the long way. I took his arms and pulled them out to his side. I made an X on both his hands with the little chalk things. He looked at me. I put the big 4 by 4 on the 4 by 6 on the floor, yanked out my big mallet, and started whacking it together. *Whacckkk!*

He leaned forward and asked, "What are you doing?" I looked up and said, "You're Jesus Christ, aren't you?" He asked, "Why do you want to know?" I said, "Oh, nothing." *Whaaaaccckk!* I took a couple of those nails and put one on one end table and one on the other, looked at his hands, and drooled a little out of the corner of my mouth. I looked at him and said, "I'm Jewish! Easter is on its way. In fact, it will be Good Friday tomorrow. Ha Ha Ha." The guy said, "Wait a minute here! I'm schizophrenic! This is just a mental disorder." I yelled, "They always say that!"

That's when they beep the doctor and shout, "I'm cure!, I'm cured! Get me out of here!" Selling cars would be a lot easier.

When they talk about schizophrenia they always say that schizophrenics went out of touch with reality. Then they try to put them in touch with reality. As a physicist I knew that we can't find "reality." I figured to make whatever they believed real. If patients believe the CIA chases them, call the CIA to come over to chase them. For me that's true.

Real Enjoyment

To some degree we all have schizophrenia *when we believe we can't* enjoy something. Many of us don't enjoy whatever we do for a living. We go there everyday. Sane.

Yet we enjoy idiotic things. People enjoy jumping out of an airplane. Think about it. Saturday they have a day off. What do they do? They go in an airplane and jump out. They think "Go out and party my ass off or jump out of an airplane? Hummm, let's jump out of an airplane!"

Some people let other people drag them behind a boat on a string while they stand on a pair of sticks…for fun! We used to call that keelhauling. It was a form of punishment.

Some people feel *thrilled* by collecting stamps. *Thrilled to the bone!* They need to have a magnifying glass to look at them. When one differs from another it *excites the hell* out of them!

Now, think about it. If you can enjoy those things, *you can enjoy anything. It's your brain!* Someone feels *motivated* to go out and jump out of an airplane? And they can't get motivated to make money??

I do a lot of training with salespeople. The idea of a client coming in and buying a car and giving them *thousands* of dollars doesn't excite them. Why? Because they daydream about *jumping out of an airplane!* You should realize *your brain* attaches the fun to it.

Trio-tuple Trance Technique

Do more for tonality. We have sound equipment. You can listen to yourself. Do auditory installation. Give yourself a smoother and more subtle tempo and tonality.

First, however, start a little exercise to put some linkage words together and to begin to do overlap. We'll do what I call a *triple induction*. We'll break into groups of four people — four humans in each group; not four people inside of each of you. The multiple-personality workshop comes next week! Those of you in literature land can start it now.

One of you will play trancee. Your job: sit there and go unconscious. Easy for most of you. Of the other three, person A will start with something visual like, "Close your eyes and make a picture where you see yourself clearly sitting in a chair going into a trance, and *as you do*..." Then stop and point to the next person, person B.

I want B to catch the tempo perfectly. I want a smooth and even rhythm. So you might say, "You're enjoying the process of seeing yourself relax *while...*" Then next person, C, catches it perfectly, not missing a beat.

Tempo is one of the most important aspects of communication. It's also one of the most unconscious. Most people overlook it.

Keep the tempo and rhythm constant so that it doesn't change when different people speak. Try to keep your tempo and intonation smooth: "He is going deeper and deeper into that kind of state *where...*" "You hear..." Keep the tempo smooth. Don't repeat the linkage word. Have a different word ready to continue the phrase. And... you can go deeper and deeper.

One of Milton's most powerful tools: he would say, "Ursala, *your unconscious...*" That's a command. That's all it is. And Milton repeated it. He said, "*Your unconscious* mind does not know much about what you're doing now, and your unconscious learning, but mostly *your unconscious*, now..."

I want you to sit down and do three rounds, okay? The first round you go visual, auditory, kinesthetic; the next round auditory, visual, kinesthetic. Try using different ones.

It is vitally important that you do not repeat their last word, the predicate they use as a linkage. So if Julius ends with the word *where* and he points, do not repeat "where." Just continue the phrase. Continue speaking as if you spoke simultaneously with him. He just happened to drop out on that word.

Remember, the content of what you say has less importance, because it's a trance induction. Content becomes important in trance *utilization.* As long as you maintain the implication that they will continue to float down on the waves of feeling that lead them deeper and deeper into an unconscious state where they can learn, really learn how to enjoy themselves, and as long as you smoothly and evenly use your tempo and tonal patterns, so that you take the words of natural language and use them to assist yourself comfortably. Now… get up and go do the exercise!

Anchoring and Post Hypnosis

When I did "The Flirting Class" I advertised it for couples. That surprised everybody. It struck me that couples have more opportunity to flirt. If they do they'll have a richer relationship.

Learn to anchor and self-anchor with hypnosis. You can add the dimension of post-hypnotic suggestion. In essence an anchor does natural post-hypnotic suggestion. "See cliff, feel fear, don't jump."

Hands go toward fire and child screams. That isn't something that's genetically built-in. When kids first see fire they go to grab it. After your hand begins to go to the fire, and your mother looks at you and goes "Ahhhhhh! Don't!" that anchors the response. Your hand starts to go out to the visual stimulus of fire. Those visual/kinesthetic responses fire off automatically.

You don't have to stick your hand in fire to learn to not to. Similarly, you don't have to get hit by a car to know not to step into the street. Human beings can learn vicariously.

Dog Trainers

Dogs can do it pretty well. Dogs learn quicker than some people. Especially the one I had. I had the smartest dog you could ever imagine. If I'd had NLP trainers like him it would have been easy.

One day I figured out that I worked for my dog. I came home after teaching all day. I had to drive two hours to get home. I walked in the door. My dog was sacked out on the couch watching television. I looked at him and I looked at my briefcase and I thought, "Something's not right here." He looked at me and said, "Hey Rich, would you go into the kitchen and fix me some food? I'm hungry." After he ate he asked me to get up and open the door. Then he could go outside to use the bushes. I thought, "What is this, I work for a dog?" The world has little twists in it. How many of you have a dog? Do you work for it or not? You go to work. They stay home and watch TV all day.

I put my dog to work. I taught him how to train people. It's a good technique. I had a German Shepherd. I used to bring him into sessions. Some clients wouldn't do what I wanted. I gave him a signal. He growled at them. They became very cooperative. I'd say, "Go into trance." The dog would go "Arrrrhh!" They'd close their eyes right away.

When a lot of people do hypnosis, they do something I have always found totally ludicrous. They fight the war of eye closure. They spend forty-five minutes trying to get somebody close-eyed. It seems like such a waste of time when you can just look at somebody and say, "Would you close your eyes?" Get down to more useful things.

The Swish in Hypnosis

Now I'll show you another little technique you can use. Some of you may have read about it. We call it the swish pattern. You take one image, and replace it with another rather rapidly.

Stop right now and think of a time and place where you felt something immensely pleasurable. When I tell people to close their eyes and think of something from their past, most people go back and pick a piece of shit. Especially therapists. They find a trauma. We don't. We go for ecstasy, pleasure and things like that. If you had a bad experience, figure "Once is enough."

I know a lot of people spend a lot of time reliving their childhoods. I didn't like mine. Once was enough.

Close your eyes and go back to a pleasant memory that you have. See what you saw at the time, hear what you heard, and literally step inside the memory so you begin to recapture the feelings. The minute you do that I want you to make a small circle in the center of this image. Have it open up and see yourself feel twice as much pleasure and be twice as happy as you've ever been. As it begins to open up enough to see it I want you to *whooshhhh* and suddenly open it up really big and wide and step inside it. Do that again and again. Keep repeating the process. It will begin to pump up your ability to *feel pleasure* more intensely and to enjoy the process of living.

Now, you can add the dimension of *where* you'd like to feel more pleasure in your life. What kinds of things would you like to enjoy? For example, see yourself enjoying the process of learning to do deep trance work.

The Joy of Competence

Some of you looked pretty serious yesterday. But you can be cured of that as well. There's much too much seriousness in the world and not enough fun.

Learn to enjoy your work. Start looking forward to going to work and using these techniques. You'll only get better at them.

Seriousness breeds incompetence. People who had prestige and no skills invented degrees. They let you have a few letters after your name and not know what you're doing. If you take that seriously, take some serious enjoyment instead.

One guy said to me that he didn't realize I went to college *forever*. I didn't get out of college until I was thirty years old. I don't hang the degrees after my name. He said, "Well, all this is well and good for you to say, but what authority do you have to be teaching us these techniques?" And I told him, "Skill." He looked at me: "Oh, that! Anybody can have skill, but do you have any degrees?" I have degrees in physics, chemistry and different things. I started telling him all the different degrees I have. Then he wanted to learn from me.

I don't want to learn something from somebody who went to school forever. I want to learn from somebody who can do it. When I designed pistol training for the army, for example, I went and found the ten best shooters, not the people with the ten most badges.

I want to see this change begin. Put emphasis on people who can do things. In psychology they had no technology. They had a lot of theory going around. They had lots of theoretical approaches. We could tell somebody to do something useful.

If a phobic walks in and says, "I'm afraid of an elevator," you should think, "How do you fix that?" Instead they would go, "Ah! Vhy ist it dot vay?" And they start asking people about their dreams, "Do you have fish in your dreams?" If you had fish in your dreams, that would explain everything.

See, I figured early on that I know why people have problems. There are only two reasons. They're born; they grow up. If it wasn't for that, you wouldn't have problems. Now we know the reasons for problems. How do you educate people to get beyond them?

Somebody in here said they read about how to cure a phobia, but they wanted to see it done. First try what's in the book to find out if it works. People all over the world use that technique. Some people just do it and it works.

A gentleman in here said something to me yesterday when I was explaining how I anchor. He said he noticed that I do it at the midline. When I said midline, the guy thought, "So that's what the midline is." When he read the book, he thought midline meant the waist. That's a legitimate mistake.

But you look for congruence at the midline. Congruence, geometrically, refers to matching on either side of a line. If you look for people to match his way, they have to grow another pair of eyes down there. It must have been tough for him to understand what I was saying.

IV

Non-Verbal
Hypnotic Inductions
Patterned Interruptions

Today we'll start with some non-verbal hypnotic inductions, because, now that you're all conscious and awake, we'll have to put an end to that. Did you have a good night's sleep? Pleasant dreams? Are you ready for some rapid inductions? By the way, I think you'll find rapid inductions to be lots of fun. Didn't you?

I want to teach you one I saw Milton Erickson do. When I met Milton, he was in a wheelchair. In fact, one of his hands didn't work. He always lifted up his right hand with his left. But Milton was an old faker too.

One of my grad students, Steve, nearly worshiped Milton. So I brought Steve down to meet him. As young kids do, he tried to put one over on Milton. Why take somebody who's got fifty years experience on you and try to screw with him in his own game? But Steve was a brash kid.

When Steve walked in, as Milton turned around and looked, Steve started to imitate him. Milton took his paralyzed hand and lifted it to shake hands with Steve. As he did he said, "I'm sorry, I didn't get your name?" Then he held out his paralyzed arm. Steve's hand went out to shake hands. Just before their hands met, Milton let his hand pass a little bit further and said, "Eyes closed now." Steve's eyes closed. "Now, I'm going to tell you a story about a boy that had bad manners," Milton said, "speaking to you as a child, now."

What a great hypnotic induction for age regression! I've seen people struggle to get back through the years. Milton just looked at him and said, "Speaking to you as a child, now, there are many times when your parents gave you a spanking. Can you feel that now?"

I thought, "Ooohhh! This old boy has got some chops! I'm going to have to remember this one!" My daughter reached an age too old for me to spank. Never have a hypnotist as a father. I go into the kitchen and see the dishes piled up. I turn around and look at her and raise one eyebrow. She says, "I'll do them; I'll do them!" There's nothing worse than getting spanked without being touched. You only have to give one and then have them relive it.

I found good use for reliving early childhood traumas. Training teenagers! I used to work in a place for juvenile delinquents. They start out with an attitude.

Their attitude starts with leaning back excessively in chairs. When I see that, I take a little hot coffee, lean over them, and drop it on their laps. They sit up straight. As they sit up you just pop them in the forehead and tell them "Sleep!" It's a one-two punch.

Then you begin inducing a state where you have *remote control*. I've worked with shoplifting. You can install a post-hypnotic suggestion. They reach for something they don't plan to pay for. Their own hands slap them in the face. It's one thing to tell someone to knock it off; it's another to tell them they're going to find it a real slap in the face.

People often talk about being of *two minds*. This manifests itself in representation systems. People say, "Well, I feel I shouldn't steal, but sometimes I see something that I just have to have." When people speak, if you tune in, you can discover how they split. Get the unconscious to align with the conscious to realize their best interests.

One of my colleagues, who works with teenagers, takes them on tours of prisons. It's one thing to think about prison; it's another to be there. He actually pays the prisoners to be abusive. That's their job! He gives them a carton of cigarettes if they're big enough assholes.

Embed Commands

I'll show you an induction, actually a couple of different ones, and then have you try some non-verbal inductions. A lot of times verbal inductions get more resistance. People consciously notice verbal inductions. Many people start out with fears about going into a trance—especially the more naive clients.

I've had people come in and say, "You can do anything to me, but don't hypnotize me." I say, "Okay, we won't *use hypnosis*. Now, I want you to close your eyes, and as long as your eyes are closed you can't *go into a trance* too deeply, and I don't want you to go into a trance *just yet* because I don't want you to *go into a trance...*"

I want you to hear the verbal pattern called *embedded command*. I began to use the technique there. Take anything you want to say and either change the tone or volume of your voice and *mark out messages*.

Milton absolutely mastered this. He would literally sway from side to side and mark the messages out in space. He would say, swaying side to side, "Now...when you *go into a trance*, you're able to learn things that *you're unconscious of* and realize just how much of a benefit they'll be when you *go into a trance* because I want you to be able to do this *now*..."

Milton didn't use as much vocal control. I don't know why. According to Earnest Rossi, Milton was, besides being color blind, both atonal and arrhythmic. He made up for it exquisitely by using positions in space. Whether you mark spatially or with a volume or tonal shift, the unconscious portions of people know a command. Get the inflection of your voice to go down so that you open up that command mode. You can look at people and say, "In a moment I want you to begin from *scratch* because nobody *knows*...because you'll soon find it *handy* and *uplifting* to learn really..." That's right, control that sensation: start from *scratch*, and nobody *knows*.

It's great, because people start sitting on their hands. Right? Either that or they go, "Well, I didn't do this!" The old hand under the nose. "Now what's he talking about?" The thing is, the command starts with "scratch" because nobody "knows." And you'll find it *irritating*...

Embedded commands don't trick people. They make the difference between you and the furniture.

Human Response—Our Glory!

I used to go to a place called Esalen. I loved to torture the people at Esalen. They are the real holdouts in the human potential movement.

Enjoy being responsive. Go ahead and scratch. Get it over with. When you don't like your response, do change it. And the best time to do that is ahead of time. If somebody always makes you angry, the best time to change it is not when you're angry. Program yourself before, so the same thing will make you alert and amused. Change it for things that work better.

Human beings can respond to just about anything in any way. Think about my examples yesterday. Some people *enjoy* jumping out of an airplane! Some people make a hobby of swimming the English Channel. Think about it! I don't know what you say when you look at ice cold water. Their bodies say, "Jump in it!" I say, "Sex, rock 'n' roll—ice cold water?" Human beings do some wild things for fun.

A big thing now: climb mountains for fun! People climb up so high they have to have an oxygen mask to breathe. Every once in a while someone gets killed. Surprise!

I see cliffs shaped like the prow of a ship. People hang off the bottom of them. You can see it on the news, "There was an accident!" There wasn't an accident. The guy did something stupid! When you see a cliff like that, your brain should say, "Walk around it!"

One of the guys in NLP is *charging* people to walk across hot coals. Didn't their parents tell them something? Me, I got a steak, a couple of potatoes, and an ear of corn, threw them on the fire, and sat on the side. I loved what Robert Dilts did. He strapped a pork chop to each foot. He walked across. Then he looked to see if the chops cooked or not.

Make people smart enough to walk around hot coals. You can overcome a fear. That doesn't mean you have to overcome a fear of doing something dumb. It's not enough that they walked across coals to prove they could overcome fear. Now it's prestigious. It's got to be a longer firewalk and it's got to be more times. People say, "I've done the firewalk seventeen times." I say, "What's the matter, didn't make it yet?"

When I'm there no one will walk across hot coals. I have a tendency to yell, "Stop!!" and "Simon says, 'Ouch!'" I love this stuff.

You can get humans to do about anything, except something useful. That's hard. Develop responses worth using.

Resistant Induction Demonstration

I want to teach you a couple of non-verbal inductions. I want to teach you the one Milton used. I used the same one yesterday. Will you come up here? You look like you're ready for this.

Yesterday I forgot to tell you the end of this. Milton brought a guy up from the audience who said, "There's no such thing as hypnosis. There's no such thing as hypnosis. Hypnosis doesn't exist." Milton said, "Well, would you come up here, sir, and prove there's no such thing as hypnosis?"

As the guy walked up, Milton said, "What did you say your name was sir? Now look at your hand and notice the changing focus of your eyes as you begin to take a deep breath and relax and close your eyes, now. That's right. And let your hand go down only at the speed that you are ready to learn something of importance to yourself and no faster. And stop right there.

That's right. Because I want you to go back in your memory and find a feeling that feels ever so good. And with each breath I want you to go deeper and deeper and enjoy the process of knowing you can learn from your unconscious, right *now*. "That's right. And as that hand goes down ever so slowly, moving only one neuron at a time, I want your unconscious to take that good feeling right here and begin to make it spread. That's right. Really learning about going into a trance ever so deeply."

How Rapid Induction Works

This is my idea of a rapid induction. Some things make any rapid induction work. Take a single activity, a behavior on automatic-pilot.

When you walk up to somebody on the street, you don't have to think about how to shake hands. It's programmed. When you go like that, his hand goes there. It knows what to do.

If you interrupt an activity like that in the middle, it's not completed. There's nothing in the middle. It's a blank.

Create ambiguity. "Do you get the *point* to the wall." That's punctuation ambiguity. The word "point" begins and ends a sentence.

For the handshake interrupt, as the other person's hand comes up, you form a cup with your thumb and first finger. Instead of meeting their right hand with yours, you put your hand in cup form under their hand coming to shake. Just gently cup it and move their hand up in front of their eyes and say, "Look!"

Handshake Demonstration

Since there's no hand-to-hand contact, there's no program. You *create the program* by passing their hand in front of their eyes and saying, "Look!" and pointing with your other hand.

Sir? Look at your hand and notice the changing focus of your eyes as you take a deep breath and relax and close your eyes and go all the way into a trance. They're looking for a program. You just fill one in.

That's right, just close your eyes. I'll let you know when you're ready. I don't want you to come halfway out; in a moment I want you to take a deep breath and let your hands go all the way down 'cause you're not done yet. You came up here and you're entitled to your present, a little present from your unconscious, *now*. That's right.

Now, I want your unconscious to pick one thing in life, one moment when you felt the most wanton courage; we call it "guts." Pick the one time when you felt that strongly about anything, where you felt…where you could just do it and do it well no matter what it was. A moment where you knew you had the strength and the courage and the charisma to just *take a hold of the moment* and really *make* things come out your way.

What I want you to do now is take that feeling and let it grow and spread and get stronger. Make the image bigger and brighter and closer. Take that feeling and, in the middle of the image, I want you to open up an image where you see yourself doing hypnosis with people, dramatically and congruently, and you feel good. In a moment I'm going to reach over and touch your hand, and as you slowly come out of trance that feeling is going to stay with you. And every single time you do something with a client that feeling will begin to spread throughout your body. That's right. There you go. And you look at the world, and you say, 'Your ass is mine!'

Handshakes All Around Exercise

Now remain conscious for just a minute for another thing. This technique, known as the handshake interrupt, breaks into a couple of pieces. One is, hand out. But then your hand goes back just a little bit—don't pull it way back, just an inch. The other hand goes behind the wrist so that it goes up; this hand points at the client's hand and you go, "*Look!* Notice the changing focus..." Thank you.

Now I'd like you to get together with two partners. Get into groups of three to try this.

It works standing up. It also works sitting down. I recommend you sit down the first couple of times. Suppose you do it standing up, and you say, "Look at your hand and notice the changing focus of your eyes as your body becomes stiff and rigid." They'll drop right on the floor. Of course, Milton did that sort of thing. He did the handshake interrupt and told a guy to sit all the way down. No chair.

Hesitation Cured

As long as they go in trance, do *layering*. Human beings, if you don't give them enough to learn, don't learn well. If you give them too much, they learn extremely well.

Each of the exercises we did yesterday had three, five or seven pieces. I walked around and checked. You guys do great.

I used to teach pieces one at a time. When I made people do just one, everybody made it more complicated. If I give them three or four, they don't. I do this in your own best interest!

Once you have them in trance, have them go and find what we call four-tuples. A four-tuple is simply a represented experience. A four-tuple includes four representational systems. Tell people to go back and see what they saw at the time, hear what they heard, feel what they felt, take a breath and notice what they could smell. Get all the sensory systems going. The more sensory systems you get going, the more changes you get to see.

Now I want you to go back and find three things, all of which will make it easier for your clients. Not only is it good to have skill as a hypnotist, but you also have to *have the right state*. NLP was developed by a madman. Its techniques were developed by people with the attitude that you have to go for things. You can't just take techniques. You've got to take *the attitude* as well, or you have to learn technique from someone else.

Now find three different times and places in your life where you *operated without hesitation*. Hesitation interferes with skill, and life in general. It's one of three major diseases. There's too much seriousness, too much hesitation, and too little lust in the world. If we took out the first two and added the third, people would get a lot more done and enjoy things a lot more.

Find three different experiences where people showed that attitude. Pick a place where you had no need to wait, where you just *got it done, now*. Find a place where you were just panting to get on with it!

The Hypnotic Multitone

Now I'll tell you a little secret. When I first studied hypnosis, almost every book I read said, "Use the monotone." Eventually I figured out why.

When I do hypnosis I find that if I say "frightened" I want to sound frightening; if I say "outrageous" I want to sound outrageous. The more congruent the message the better it works.

Yet when I saw most hypnotists I found that their monotone proved useful for them. They were maximally incongruent. They'd say "Deeper and deeper asleep?" That's like turning to somebody and asking, "How do you feel about that?" with your eyes looking up, or saying, "Looks good to me!" with eyes going down and left. Ouuuhhh! Gives you the creeps, doesn't it?

To do incongruence, say things and act the opposite. Say "I want you to relax." in a voice that would galvanize Stephen King. Whine, "Feel comfortable in your seat all the way down," while you wince. It does not have a positive impact.

You can make each and every word sound like what you mean. When you say "relax," do more than say the word. You want your tonality to sound like what you say. When you talk about "regret," *sound* like regret. When you talk about "relaxing, feeling comfortable," make those words a massage. When you talk about "smoothing out difficulties" take those words and use them as a tool.

Get the maximum effect out of each word. When you talk about "courage," sound like you mean it. When you talk about "wanton ecstasy" make sure your voice sounds like what you talk about. It's not the number of words you say or how fast you say them. It's how much impact you get out of each word.

The trick to layering responses really works quite simply. You find memories and resources one by one. While they're in trance, have them go back to each. Then you stack them together.

Honest Hypnosis

In trance you can use age regression. Have them look at past events, remembering the time and place they want to go back to. As they do, have the present disappear so that the past becomes more real. Now they can go back *honestly* to that time.

"Honestly" is a semantically loaded word. Honestly means completely. It also applies moral leverage. In trance, the unconscious *understands semantic totality* of words such as "honestly." It doesn't understand polite language.

When people go into trance, you *must be very literal* with them. The part of the mind that processes what we call conversational postulates and implications simply does not function.

Say to somebody in trance, "Can you remember it now, honestly and completely. See what you saw, hear what you heard, feel what you felt at the time and let it spread so that you're still there fully; see what you saw intensely. Do it more intensely than you did at the time."

Post Hypnotic Anchors

Take someone back to each of those events. Give the person this post-hypnotic suggestion: "When I touch you like this, you'll be able to reexperience these feelings fully."

I want you to use three different fingers to make three different anchors. You can fire all three at the same time later on. You'll do something like what we did yesterday.

Then bring them back to the present: "I want you to come back to the present time and I want you to think about using these techniques, doing handshake-interrupts, doing NLP, doing hypnosis, wherever you're going to use them; with your clients, your neighbors, your loved ones, your friends. As you do, each time I want you to take this, and then fire all three anchors, so that you..."

Many hypnotists have done what we call "wussy" hypnosis. When they think about using a technique, they don't go for it. That hesitation comes across in their voices.

If you do pain control, you don't want to pussyfoot around. If you stick a pin through someone's hand, you don't want half-ass hypnosis. I did pain-control for the army. One of the guys doing the training with me was a little bit incongruent. He said, "And you're not going to *feel this pain.*" That's not the command you want to give. That's like, "Don't think of blue or green."

Post Anaesthetic Anchoring

The last time I went to the dentist, he grabbed my mouth, took out the hypodermic needle and said, "Now this is going to hurt a little bit." And I went, "Arrgghhh!" I had just done forty-five minutes of pain control and this guy gives me a suggestion that I'm going to feel pain?! I don't need that at all.

People go into trance when you hold a hypodermic needle in front of their faces. Do we have any dentists in here? Or doctors? Have you ever noticed? It's the fastest induction I know. In fact, I use it with some of my clients. I do sales work. If they won't sign the contract, I pull out a big hypodermic needle, grab part of the inside of their mouth like this and ask, "Do you want to sign it or what?" You'd be surprised.

Go ahead and try this. Grab someone's mouth the way the dentist does. You can demonstrate that the human body can learn. You know how the dentist grabs the inside of your cheek? He pulls it straight out and wriggles it up and down. So grab the inside of your mouth and pull like this. Now wait a minute and notice what happens. Do you want to talk about an anchor? Numbs up, doesn't it?

Dentists do that all the time. They've already got the anchor. They start adding the suggestions: "It's beginning to get a little more numbness." For some of you it's beginning to spread to the side of your tongues. Do you know what I mean? Can you feel that intensifying now?

Insofar as you replicate the touch that the dentist used with you, it will reinduce that state. If the dentist does it the same way, it will reinduce the drug state. In *Applied Neurodynamics* I show you how to reinduce drug states fully. You can go all the way in.

Highway Consciousness

Just don't do it while you drive! This one thing scares the shit out of me. I've been selling hypnosis tapes. Once, when I had somebody pick me up at the airport, they had fifteen of my hypnosis tapes in the car. I thought, "Oh my God!" I'm going to put a label on them: "Do not operate machinery while listening to these tapes." I can just see this person driving, and hear myself, "Now let your eyes close all the way."

In this town that person wouldn't last five minutes. It's one thing driving down a country road, but here people are at war! It's a good thing they don't have more guns. In L.A. they shoot people on the freeways. It's a big thing now. Just a way of saying hello. Keeps people on their toes.

Do you know what this has done in L.A.? It made everybody *real polite* when they drive. People used to just cut anybody off. But some people started shooting if they got cut off. Other people got real sweet. You never know who's in the next car.

Knowing Why

Start out with an induction by trying the handshake-interrupt. You'll find that rapid inductions work nicely. I'll show you a couple more so you have a little variation. It can be a little awkward at first. For example, decide which of you will do it.

I initially modeled all these geniuses for two reasons. I wanted to do what they did, and it seemed ridiculous that an entire field didn't have any skills in it. The field of psychology boiled down to that.

In California, people sat in hot tubs. They talked a great game. They said, "Well, now you're talking out of your parent, now you're talking in your child, and now in your adult." Great inductions, but if you get people into trance, you need to do something with it. Why get somebody to have more bad internal dialogue? People still walk around in California cringing from their internal dialogues. They tell themselves they shouldn't be telling themselves anything.

You can completely give up making pictures in your head and talking to yourself. We call it death. Having consciousness is called thinking. One thing in the world that I don't want to eradicate is thinking.

I noticed that in the human-potential movement at Esalen. A lot of people there, for example, didn't know they were naked. I went to Esalen and got to those beautiful tubs down by the ocean. Everybody took off their clothes. I sat in this tub and looked at this lady and said, "Great tits!" Suddenly she knew she was naked. I guess she missed it or something. They all took off their clothes and tried to pretend they weren't naked. It didn't make any sense to me. I know when I'm naked. And I know why.

The next trick is to anchor each of these responses. You will have three separate anchors. Make sure that you anchor each one with a different finger so that you can, ultimately, fire them all.

Then bring the person back to the present. Associate it with where they need it. When you bring him to the present, where they need it, fire the resource anchors.

After that, give straight-ahead post-hypnotic suggestions. They're free. When bringing clients out of trance I lay it on thick. I tell them they're going to be healthier, they're going to be happier in every part of their lives; their sexual potency is going to increase. I figure you might as well throw it all in. The more you keep layering that stuff on and the more sessions you do with a client, the more those things seep into their lives.

In one seminar that Eric Robbie and I did, we put everybody into a trance, oriented them to the future and had them pick lottery numbers. Do they have a lottery here? Maybe we'll try that.

"Did it work?"

As a matter of fact, a couple of them won between three and five thousand dollars. It's not a bad deal; you go to a seminar and make money. Those who really worked at trance work won the money. The people who were doing all the the serious language patterns, grammar and that stuff, they didn't win a cent. Actually, that's about what they did win.

Last Handshake

Before you break into groups of three, let me show you one more time how to do this. Get the hand movement. Sir, will you come up here for a minute?

Remember to practice it when you start out. After you've learned this pattern, follow through and do the trance work. First, get the movement smooth.

The movement is: hand out, pause, backward movement, drop fingers underneath, one movement in front and point. Then say, "Trance, close eyes..." See, it works! It's okay; it means you're not a piece of furniture.

Your other hand will go like this—sweeping across the face while this hand follows with finger pointing, and you say "Look...at your hand! Notice the changing focus of your eyes as you take a deep breath and just relax and let your eyes close now, that's right! And as you do, enjoy the sensation of relaxing and knowing that you can learn with your unconscious."

The fact that human beings can respond is what makes them special and *alive*, that's what makes them have happiness and joy, that's what gives them sexual prowess. I can talk to a chair but it does not respond. When you talk to human beings, the degree to which they're able to respond is the degree to which they're able to learn, and that's what makes them so special. That's what makes life fun.

In a moment I'm going to touch you at the midline and when I do, you'll start to come out of the trance, feeling wonderful and really ready, and inside your head you'll say to the world, "Your ass is mine!" That's right. All the way up now. Ummmmm! Yeah!

V

The House-Cleaning Pattern
The Redoubtable Belief Mobile

Most of the time I only see a client once. So I developed a way to do what I call cleanup work. Even if I make only one change with a person they very often start thinking about ninety other things to change. Many times people hand me a list of things to deal with. One guy had thirty pages.

Distinguish two kinds of change. One is remedial change. Fix what went wrong. We can do better than that.

Psychology itself grew out of the medical model. That model dominates the field of psychology. The medical model is remedial. People primarily go to a doctor when they are sick. When you fall down and break your arm you go to a doctor and say, "Fix it."

Freud, coming from a medical background, thought in terms of the remedial model. He thought in terms of "What went wrong? What is broken? How do we fix it?" Freud did marvelous work for his time. His distinctions about unconscious processes were brilliant for that day and age.

The problem is the same in all fields. People often confuse one man's brilliant work with, "That's all there is." Today we use new distinctions.

When I first came into psychology people gave me strange looks. I said, "Computer science can do more in terms of change work for people." Here I was, a twenty-three year old kid. Most of the people in the field thought computer technicians were insensitive and boring.

For instance, what do most people think about me when they read *The Structure of Magic*, or, that true sleeper, *NLP Volume I?* That's the best sedative to knock you out at night. Actually, *The Structure of Magic* was my dissertation.

You can't put *any* humor in a dissertation. They won't accept it. Those people have been in college too long. They think, "If you tell jokes, that means it doesn't work or, if it does, it shouldn't.

So my dissertation, *The Structure of Magic*, was not accepted. The problem, however, was that "Who's Who" put me in for it. I was the first person at the college to get in. The college wanted the plaque. So they went ahead and passed me. Isn't that ridiculous?

When I went to college, I only did badly in two courses. I got a D in Psych 101 and I flunked public speaking. What do I end up doing for a living? Talking to psychologists!

I went back to my college years later. I went to my psych professor and said, "It turned out that I was right." She said, "What do you mean?" I said, "You know all those answers I answered wrong? I was right! Now you have to read my book to pass the test. So I want my grades changed." She looked at me and said, "Does the phrase 'too late' mean anything to you?"

I have more interest in the second kind of change—generative change. People do this anyway. It's called "growing up." People unconsciously develop on their own.

So think less about change as remedial. Think more of change as generative. We can even orient people in this way. The way I do this is simple. Do the first part of it before they go into trance.

Part I: Sorting Out

This pattern will help you do two really valuable things. First it will enable you to get rid of your garbage. Then it will empower you to make your resources more real and present to you. This will give you more power and choice.

First, think of something that's true of you, and you love it. Find a specific example. Elicit the submodalities of this strong belief or self-understanding. Identify its submodalities.

Second, pick something which you know was you, but it doesn't seem like you anymore. This representation of yourself simply doesn't fit the you of today. Also, find the submodalities of this representation.

I did things as a teenager. When I think about them now, I can't believe I did them. I can't believe I lived through them. But you know I did.

For you, to do this, stop and remember something from your youth. Find, somewhere in your life, things that you used to do.

Find things that, when you think about it now, you know it was you doing it, but it doesn't feel like it was you.

Perhaps it was a belief. Are there any beliefs that you had when you were younger? Like, "Candy is the most important thing in the world!" And perhaps now you can't even stand to eat it? We all change anyway. Whether we have a therapist or not, we change. People change in spite of therapy.

Third, compare and note the differences of submodalities. How do the two representations differ? Do a thorough contrastive analysis of these two representations. Perhaps the images of the two representations will have different places in your mind, or a different size, different brightness, different closeness. One may be a movie, the other a slide. It might be in color, or black and white. Go down the list of submodality possibilities.

Ignore similarities. Note the differences. List them systematically.

Pay special attention to association and dissociation. You'll usually find profound differences there. This distinction exists in all systems.

Check this separately for each system. In associated visual memory, you see what you saw at the time, out of your own eyes, the same way you saw it at the time; dissociated, you see yourself. In the auditory system, the difference between association and dissociation lies in whether you can hear what you heard in the event, or whether you have talk about it. In kinesthetic association, you actually feel as if you go back into the sensations of your body again; in memories in kinesthetic dissociation you don't have those same feelings that you had in your body. You can't get the feelings back. It doesn't feel like it's you anymore. Do not plan to find absolute distinctions. You will find some dissociations on a continuum.

Pay attention to the location of sounds. How close? Notice whether it moves and if it sounds like it's going out or whether it sounds like it's coming closer.

Pay attention to the duration of the memory. If it's a movie, how long does it last? Does it run at the same speed as life?

This all prepares for impactful change. Methodically elicit the internal structure. Get the critical submodality differences. Write them out on paper. On the right side put "This is true of me." On the left put, "This is not true of me any longer." That will assist you later.

Fourth, begin building a generative hypnotic system out of these submodalities. Design this system for yourself, and later your clients, to keep making changes. You'll set up a system where a person can make ten changes every week. So I call it "Housecleaning."

Are there not behaviors that you need to get rid of? Aren't there things that don't serve you anymore? This has proven especially valuable for people who kept whining about childhood. Fifty-year-old people can whine about how their parents treated them. That's time to give it up. There's nothing you can do about it now. Except this.

Part of growing up, and getting on with your own life, comes in realizing that, "Yes, the events I've lived through are how I've learned to be who I am." And part of maturity is in letting go of junk. And you can do that simply by throwing it into the garbage can! Here's how.

Part II: Building the Grid in Trance

Fifth, induce a trance. You have methodically transcribed the differences between the "It is true of me" representation and the "It is no longer true of me and no longer fits" representation. Do a handshake interrupt, or any quick induction. Induce a deep trance.

Then embed, inside of the person, the ability to take both sets of submodalities and to create a grid out of them. You can do this. Hold the submodalities constant and *take the content out.*

For instance, let's say that what's true of you is an image on the right side and what's not true of you any longer is on the left side. The first is larger; the second is smaller. The first is a movie; the second is a slide. The first is associated; the second is dissociated. Take these submodalities and *set up a grid.*

Just turn the brightness up. Hold the other submodalities still. Turn it up until the representation completely whites out. It will then have no content. But it's still in the same place. This works for a visual lead. With the auditory system, turn the sound all the way down, or all the way up till it blows out, then stick in new content, then turn it up again. *That creates the grid.*

Why lead visually and auditorally? We're creating a feeling. We thus use the auditory and visual systems to lead the kinesthetics.

Have you noticed how peoples' emotions get in their way in life? If you learn as a child to be afraid of strangers—that might be useful, or it might not. As an adult you have to go out and meet people. Fear of strangers becomes paranoia in the extreme. That might be a behavior you want to put here to dispose of. You might want to substitute, "I am curious about people" as a new self representation.

Sixth, put in new content. Put onto the white grid something that the person would like to be true of themselves. Use something that's almost true, but not quite. For instance, "I am becoming a skilled hypnotist." With the new representation there, turn the brightness down to normal. Leave the grid there and put in new content.

Seventh, trash the unwanted behaviors. Start with the representation about the past, the thing no longer true. Turn the brightness up until it whites out. Then turn it back down. Have the old image fall right out the back and have it fall into a trash can so that you can hear the sound of compacted trash landing in that garbage can. Boom! Internal auditory anchors can work very powerfully. As soon as you finish that, stick in your next belief to change, "Strangers will hurt me," or whatever.

Grid Debriefing

What comments do you have about the exercise? I noticed that some of you had problems getting answers from your clients. I want you to realize that you can elicit specific distinctions. It boils down to asking, "How do you know?" All submodality distinctions come from getting specific information. If a person has a belief, they believe one thing as opposed to another. How do they know which?

Some of you let your clients go off into drivel. When you ask a person to make a distinction as to whether the picture is bigger or smaller and they start telling you about their childhood, use the phrase, "Shut up!" Say, "I don't want to hear it." Tell them, "Look at one, look at the other, tell me which is larger or smaller."

Communication can boil down to a trance war. How many therapists go to work feeling good and return home feeling like shit? Why? Because the client says, "I thought things were going good, but I look back and feel bad" and then they reach over, touch and say, "You know what I mean?" The therapist says, "Yeah, I can feel that." Clients say, "I thought my husband really loved me, but he didn't do that, and it makes me feel bad." So I do a lot of secret therapy. I don't want clients inducing their problems in me.

Protect yourself from the onslaught of bad suggestions. If people got themselves into a stuck state, they can do the same to you. I want to hear about the good stuff. I let them talk to me once they have a state of ecstasy. In bad states, don't listen for content. Listen to find out when they know to be depressed.

Depressives have as many good experiences and as much fun as the rest of us. Their structured way of looking back gives them bad feelings. Their way of looking through history makes it look depressing. They take good events and shift them into the submodalities of depression—a backwards swish.

Find out how they do it wrong. Get them to knock it off. Shift it the other way; the other way.

Gusto Group Hypnosis

Now since you've all done so well, as a little present, close your eyes, relax, and say to yourself, 'My ass is gone!' ... into a trance, now, deeply and smoothly and comfortably and take all the good feelings that you can find within you and the satisfaction and the knowledge... that you've been learning both consciously and unconsciously... because one of the things I do while I teach is I convey a lot to the conscious mind because I believe conscious minds are smart, basically, and that they are good learners.

But simultaneously I deliver a lot of unconscious messages... and learnings, and I know that your unconscious has picked up on a lot of that. And I want you to go inside and to ask your unconscious to assist you in learning exquisitely how to have these skills come out of you slowly, in the days and weeks ahead, so that you learn to be methodical about communication, and you learn to trust your ability to see what's working and what's not working. To try new things, to do new things...

You see, all these techniques will work with your pets, they'll work with your friends, they'll work with your lovers and lovers-to-be. But one of the things that I want you to know is that it's okay to take this and go and use it to make your life happier. You can do it to increase your capacity to be compassionate and to make the people around you compassionate.

And you can also use it to make more money. You can use it to close more sales. Because the more money you have, the more you'll be able to give to others. I know that many of us in the human-potential movement developed a bugaboo about money. But, bless you my children, the cashman is here to tell you it's okay to make more money. "Sometimes when you're feeling lean, all you need is some of the green."

That's why God invented money. That's also why God invented sex and friends. Because those are the things that make you feel full. And it's okay to have mucho money and sex and to fall in love if you need to. Just don't do it too often and at the same time. It's okay to feel compassion to the nth power of your soul and it's okay to want more sex.

With that in mind, I want you to go back to the beginning of this workshop and build for yourself a cap; one that runs through all you've learned about submodalities and how to build beliefs. We used to think beliefs were amorphous things, but now you can stop and know what a belief is. Imagine what you can accomplish. Build for yourself, each night, or when you get up, two new useful beliefs. Get rid of two you don't like, and add two that you need.

Starting with a foundation of positive and joyous beliefs about the magic of life, you can begin to increase your competence and skill at whatever you do. You can learn more about language and how to use anchoring, and you can learn more from studying people who are successful in your fields. There's so much out there. Now you have the building blocks, both conscious and unconscious, to really blossom.

You can look at this as another new beginning. In life we have many of them. We learn to become adults, we learn language, we get married, sometimes we get divorced. All of these are beginnings. There are no ends in life that we know of for sure. They say that death is an end, but we're not even sure about that.

Don't worry about what can't be done or might get in the way. Start to look at whatever is possible that you want. Reach out and grab it with gusto. Look at the world and say, 'Your ass is mine!' You're going to love it.

With that in mind, I want all of those skills to solidify so what you've learned goes with you as you leave this room. I want your unconscious to be responsible for taking the learning we've built here together and make it begin to expand so that you take all the personal power you've developed here and think of it as a rosebud that's about to bloom. Because when you walk out the door I want you to sign yourself up for life, for excitement, for new learning, for falling in love with life and magic itself so that in the work you do everyday you add everything you want and need for yourself.

Align your conscious and unconscious resources so that you step out as a congruent human being and look at the world as the world's biggest smorgasbord. Life is nothing but an unprecedented opportunity to learn and grow and do new and exciting things. With that in mind, there's nothing else to say except slowly open your eyes, and, as we say where I come from, *adios.*

A System That Will Deal With Problems As They Arise

We've started to build an internal system so that when problems occur you will have a way of dealing with them. When you find yourself doing things you don't want to do, this system will enable you to get rid of those behaviors. It will give you a way of going back and finding resources that you may not have as much as you'd like.

Some of you were playful as kids. But as you grew up, the fund was beaten out of you. When I went to school they had an interesting way of attaching unpleasantness to learning. When you did something wrong they whacked you with a ruler. I was left-handed. People at my school decided I should not write with my left hand. So when I picked up a pencil with my left hand they would go *whack!*

Reprogram these kinds of negative lessons. Program in positive behavior, like being courageous. In communication, flexibility in your behavior increases your ability to elicit responses. Develop the ability to get rid of constraints that hold us back from developing greater skills and competence.

Most people consider the hypnosis we've been doing to be very difficult. They make it hard. Trance work gets easy if you concentrate on opening up the channels of comprehension. Get your tonal shifts to go down. Get people into a suggestible mode. Make yourself congruent in your communications.

Part III: Trashing the Garbage

First, stop, close your eyes, and think of ten behaviors that get in your way that you would like to get rid of. They don't have to be big ones. You can use old behavioral patterns like easily getting into a rut of doing things. You just don't need them anymore. Identify your list. It's important to let your conscious mind participate in things like this. It has strong opinions about what it wants.

You may use behaviors that you're capable of, but just don't enjoy enough. Many people can play with their dogs or kids, but when they do therapy they get serious. The more serious you get about your client's problems, the more you reinforce the idea that they have serious problems.

They may simply whine. On the other hand, I've had clients who had tragic lives. Remember they *had* tragic lives. If they keep reliving the tragedy over and over again and taking it seriously, they will keep living that way for the rest of their lives. Do the most humane thing you can do. Begin to get them to have a sense of humor about the tragedy. When they can look back and laugh they can set themselves free from the past and get on with the future.

I know people so hooked on looking for problems that they go to past lives looking for them. The issue isn't whether people have past lives; it's getting people to look forward in their present lives to what they're going to do that's useful. As they become more ferocious about living, and enjoy living more, it's just going to become a better world to live in.

Second, note your two grids. You have a grid for behaviors that you want to get rid of and one for behaviors that you like.

Double Demonstration of Application

Third, induce a state of trance. We will demonstrate with two subjects, a man and a woman.

(to the woman) Do you have your list? Good. Hold you hand up here like that. I want you to just look at your hand, and as you do I want you to notice how to take a very deep breath very slowly. That's right. And very slowly relax and allow your eyes to close.

That's right. And go all the way down, deeper and deeper still... into an altered state.

What you're doing now is the very thing you did when you first went to school and started to learn your letters and numbers. What you were doing then was building a foundation of learning that would stay with you for the rest of your life. That's right; all the way down.

(to the man) Now, floating on the waves of relaxation, go deeper with each breath, that's right, and enjoy the process. What you're doing now is just the beginning of learning and understanding and making changes in your life, changes that you'll enjoy, changes that will help you understand how to make life much more full of ecstasy. And as you continue to float down in the depths of trance, both a part of and apart from yourself with utter clarity and a growing sense of satisfaction in the knowledge that you can and will learn... really learn about going into a trance, now.

Because the process of learning about going into a trance is a rare and unprecedented opportunity for you to take the resources in the back of your mind, those unconscious resources that keep your heart beating, that keep your blood pressure down, that slow down your breathing, and that allow you to feel relaxed. I want you to allow your hand to go down only at the rate that you drop into a deeper trance than you ever thought you could go into before. Now. That's right. All the way down. Really dropping.

(to both) Because what you're going to do is let your unconscious... learn, really learn. I want your mind to begin to make the adjustments at the unconscious level, to do for you a service of much importance. You're going to assist yourself in the process of building a machine within your mind that takes the unneeded behaviors and makes them both a part of and apart from yourself with growing and wanton pleasure. That's right. And really enjoy the thought.

Because I want you to take what you did in the exercise of eliciting submodalities and assist your conscious portions in beginning to learn to be a perpetual-motion machine. Now, at the unconscious level, begin to make preparations to build an automatic machine that will kick off each night as you begin to sleep and dream. Do so by putting up those two perceptual grids. Starting on one side, put the things that you enjoy and like that are a part of you; on the other side put things that are no longer a part of you—the things that get thrown out.

I want you to take that first unwanted behavior and have it just pop into your mind. That's right. Slam it very quickly over into that area that contains things you no longer feel are a part of you. Have that behavior fall out the back and drop into the trash can; hear the sound of that metal on metal and know that it is no longer a part of you. Then you can pull up the next one and slam it into what's no longer a part of you and drop it down.

Once you've done that, I want you—between each and every thing you throw away—to pull up something that you really need to make much more true about yourself and throw it inside of where that which is true of you is. So you throw away one thing and add one thing. Throw away one thing; add one thing. Continue to do this, one right after the other. Cycle through those ten behaviors on your list until your unconscious is sure that those things you don't need will no longer plague you. The things you need more of will become the responsibility of your unconscious to have more of in your life.

When your unconscious is convinced that those ten things will no longer plague you, and that the ten new things will make your life more dynamic and powerful, then and only then do I want your unconscious to allow one of your hands to rise so that I can know you're ready for the next step. That's right.

How the System Works

In essence, we've taken the natural process of sorting things through submodalities and begun to stimulate something that would happen eventually on its own. It's like noting the difference between something you understand and something you're confused about. By comparing submodalities you can shove the thing that confused you into the submodalities of understanding. You will understand more.

This happens anyway. Some people have to sleep. When they wake up things get clearer. Sometimes it's a matter of time going by. What actually happens is that you make a shift in your own mind. For some people all their images are fuzzy and they're confused. The images are clear when they understand. If you take fuzzy images and make them clear, you will understand more.

By using these natural processes of cognition we can begin to accelerate them. This speeds up how you organize yourself internally. It gives you the opportunity to have more control over how you can make changes that will stay with you for the rest of your life.

Demonstration (continued)

(to the woman) Now, take all the time you need to make sure that all these changes are solid, and that your unconscious mind now takes full responsibility for guaranteeing that you've made these adjustments while she floats deeper and deeper and gets more relaxed. Relaxing her shoulders and neck, and all the muscles in her face, give her that internal, unconscious massage that feels so good while you make these changes. And when all these changes have solidified, one of your hands will rise so I know you're ready for the next step.

Now I know your unconscious has made all these adjustments. As a demonstration of your unconscious power, I want your unconscious to do something for you. I want this hand to float up even more until it's all the way up. That's right.

Open your palm like this. I want your unconscious, when it's ready, to allow your eyes—not yet—to open very slowly. When you open your eyes, I want you to see something surprising in your hand, something that's going to amaze you about how these adjustments will change your life. I want you to go deeper and deeper and deeper; when your unconscious knows you're ready, your eyes will open slowly. It will only deepen your trance and you will be surprised delightfully by what's in front of you. That's right. But not until she's ready.

Deeper and deeper still, getting more and more curious. That's right. And when your eyes open, you'll go deeper and deeper... and you can laugh your way all the way down. Your unconscious will know when your eyes are ready to open. Now, very slowly... There you go. What do you see? That's right. Just watch and learn. Let your unconscious show you something surprising about your future.

Take all the time you need. Now let your eyes close and drift deeply back into trance. Allow your hand to go down comfortably and slowly and let it close all the way down so that you'll keep that change right by your heart for the rest of your life.

(to the man) Now go ahead and finish and pay attention to what it's doing at the unconscious level. I'm going to reach over and lift up your hand. You can just hold it there. I'm going to stroke this finger; your unconscious can answer 'yes' by moving that finger and 'no' by lifting this finger. Just like that. Do you understand? All right. Now, have you made all the adjustments to ensure that Charlie has made these changes? All right.

And I want you to allow this hand to rise up very slowly the rest of the way, up towards his face so it begins to feel drawn, like there's a rubber band between his finger and his nose. It's sort of like the attraction to new learning, to new understanding, and as the hand gets closer and closer I want you to realize that when it touches your nose you're going to begin to dream a dream that will show you just how fine the future can be. But not until it touches your nose. At the last minute you're going to have trouble. Your arm is going to get stuck and you're going to struggle. You can try as hard as you want to touch your nose. But you'll have a problem.

It's like the battle just before you get what you want. When you struggle successfully with your own mind he'll always win. Suddenly your hand can go up the rest of the way. And when you get in touch nobody knows exactly what you'll see, but you'll find that learning and understanding will burst into your mind as you dream a vivid dream. Getting ever so close now. That's right. All the way up now; struggling and fighting until you do just a little bit of... that's right. And dream that dream. Now. That's right.

Now, very slowly, as all the learning and understanding become solidified in your future and in your mind, I want your unconscious to guarantee that all these things will drift into your behavior easily and quickly. As this hand moves down, I want your unconscious to prepare to do this every night as you drift off into sleep, with just the changes that you would like to make for yourself, that your ability to learn will get turned on every time you need it, taking away unwanted behaviors and adding new and dynamic resources. And if there are no behaviors to take away, you can just wantonly increase and enrich all the good things already there—because the process of learning never stops.

As you drift back to the conscious state your unconscious mind makes all the preparations, so when it takes responsibility for this program in the future, then and only then will you take a deep breath and sit up. Wide awake and almost alert."

The Redoubtable Belief Mobile

You all have all the raw materials needed to do this. I want you to take all your skills and become artisans. You have a chance to begin building a machine that does the change work.

We have several doctors here. Anyone dealing with difficult medical problems needs to be able to access every healing resource available. This is true no matter what kind of treatment you're using.

You might as well make patients believe it can work. It never hurts to give every positive suggestion you can. No matter what our profession, anything that helps us, helps us.

Steps Reviewed

1) Take the person all the way down into a trance. Set up finger signals until you can get him deep enough so you can get the unconscious mind to signal yes or no. Use lots of deepening techniques to take the person all the way down.

You can use the handshake interrupt, belief change, whatever you like. You can do what I did; just lift up the hand until you feel catalepsy. Then touch the person without clearly indicating where you're holding. Let your touch become light and keep shifting it from place to place so it becomes too hard to tell when you let go. Also use massive embedded commands for relaxing, sleeping, etc., to deepen the trance.

2) Ask the person's unconscious if it would set up those two grids using the list of submodality differences.

3) Then have the unconscious take the ten behaviors the person identifies and get ready the ones they don't want. For each one to get rid of, add a new resource; thus, for every void you create, you fill it with something dynamic. Get a yes signal for each pair.

4) Now have the person hallucinate a garbage can. When the behavior or belief that's no longer wanted or true falls out,

the person can hear the sound of it falling. Hear a bolt closing so that it can't come back.

5) Have the unconscious signal when it completes working with the first behavior. Take this a piece at a time, very slowly. Once the person has trashed something, have him add something. Then do the second one. Then have the unconscious go through each of the ten and give you a signal when it completes each one. Sit there and count the finger movements.

6) When the ten are completed, ask the unconscious if it will take responsibility for doing this each night as the person drifts off to sleep. This then becomes a daily routine for the unconscious to use to clean up things. This embeds an unconscious program that becomes a tool for personal change, excellence, and ecstasy. Every time the person falls asleep the unconscious works at getting rid of shit still left in his life.

This *propulsion system* can help people become more dynamic in whatever they do. People can use this at work. Whatever they're not doing well, they can tune it right up and can add more dynamic qualities to their lives. What could be better?

VI

Getting More Time
For a Change

Two hypnotic phenomena became my all-time favorites: fast and slow time distortion. We learn them today. I first learned about "time distortion" from Milton Erickson.

Unlike most people, he used it for unusual things. I met Milton later in his life. He hadn't fallen into a rut. He still created new, unexpected ways of using techniques.

He used time distortion for weight control. I know that sounds funny. I once saw Milton work with a very large woman.

He said, "The problem with you is that you eat too much." She said, "I know." Milton then replied, "And do you know why you eat too much? It's because you have too much time to eat. Now, as you sit there looking at me, you don't know if it will be now or in five minutes or when I point a finger at you, but you do know that one of those times is when your eyes will shut tightly and you'll drop into a deep, somnambulistic trance. And your conscious mind will go into a past memory, leaving only your unconscious mind to enjoy itself and to speak to me privately about matters of importance. Now."

He then had her go in so that her unconscious mind remembered the difference between time that moves quickly and time that moves slowly. He said, "When you're driving down the highway, sometimes you can drive for what seems forever. Sometimes three or four hours go by like that," snapping his fingers. "Sometimes when you're seeing a two-hour movie that you really enjoy, it seems to go by like that," snapping his fingers again. "But there is also the time that moves *very slowly*. You might be waiting in line for what seems to be an hour and you'll look at your watch and only a minute has gone by."

Then Erickson said, "I want you to go back and remember a movie you saw." He then had her watch that movie in fast time; she saw a two-hour movie in two minutes. Then he had her do something where time moved slowly. When he then had her open her eyes, she was to see a fork and a plate of food in front of her. He had her reach down towards the fork. It took an hour for her hand to get down there. It took another hour for her hand to get back up.

Now that's an unusual way of dieting. Yet if you sit down and think about it taking an hour per bite, you won't eat nearly as much. It didn't really take an hour, it just *seemed* like an hour. This takes a lot of fun out of eating, exactly what Milton had in mind. Personally, I don't want to torture my clients quite that much, unless I don't like them.

Time and Skill

You can use time distortion for lots of things. I once took a young woman of eighteen, a great hypnotic subject, put her in trance, and sped up her vision to the point where the world moved in slow motion. I then took her out on a mat and put her against a fifth-degree black belt in Aikido. Without any martial-arts training, she beat him. She had all the time in the world. He would make moves, but her movements were much faster. By the way, this is what great martial artists do anyway.

Great baseball players do it too. A baseball team once hired me. Pitchers can throw the ball more than 100 miles per hour. That sucker moves fast!

Imagine if I threw something a hundred miles an hour. Your job is to hit it. First you have to see it.

I'm an implicit modeler. I think that in order to model human skill you have to actually develop an ability to do it yourself. Teach yourself to do it yourself. Then you can start creating ways to transmit it to others.

I believe you can't model objectively. Some of my colleagues try. Some of them come out with good stuff that way. Still, for me, if your model works, you should do it.

I always start out with ignorance as my best tool and try things normally. With the baseball team, I got up at the plate and said, "Throw me some fast balls." The pitcher said, "I did." I saw his hand go back. Then I heard the sound of the ball in the catcher's mitt behind me.

Later, I talked with the team's hitters. I found out how they saw the ball. I asked about the difference between a good day and a bad day. It turns out that these guys go into a trance, slow down time and make the ball bigger. That will make hitting a lot easier.

We found the same in target shooting. The guys who do great at target shooting hallucinate the target. They move it up real close and make it real big. That makes it hard to miss. We put that in our training.

Find the trance phenomena inside of human behavior. The human brain does them anyway. Trance just gives you the ability to control them.

Hallucination Skill

People have positive and negative hallucinations. How many of you have put your car keys on a table and made them disappear? You looked on that table a hundred times. Then you realized they were right there all the time! That's a negative hallucination. Your brain did it!

I have a theory about why brains do this—it's because the earth tilts on its axis. As a result, we all have somebody else's brain. Naturally, all our brains got pissed off. Brains also have a sense of humor. So as long as the earth tilts on its axis, human beings do silly things.

Negative hallucinations actually include positive hallucinations. You have to figure out what must lie behind, say, a barstool and hallucinate that. Positive hallucinations include negative; you have to not see things behind what you imagine. You can't do just one.

Our eyes don't really see things. We see a representation built on the cortex. When you learn to do hallucinations you actually learn to create your own representations. We can actually electronically detect the response of your neurons to your imagination.

I once taught a group of college students who knew the information, but not how to take tests. They had trouble passing their medical exams. I taught them to hallucinate writing all the answers on the walls. When they took the test, they could look on the wall and write down the answers. That would be cheating except they had written them up there inside of their minds. In essence, people with good memories do that. Some people experience it inside; others on the outside.

The Skill of Schizophrenia

The usual difference between someone who hallucinates and someone who visualizes is that the person who hallucinates doesn't know he's doing it or doesn't have any choice about it. One schizophrenic I worked with hallucinated people coming out of the television set and following him around. Think about that.

When I heard this, I said, "Wow! That's great!" He looked at me and said, "What do you mean it's great?" I said, "Well, what do you watch?" He said, *"Little House on the Prairie."* On that show there's a snippy little bitch named Mary. She kept coming out of the screen and following this guy around going, "Aarrhh, aarrhhh, aarrhhh" just like she does on the program. She would bitch and moan until he would freak out and start screaming. Of course he was a paranoid schizophrenic!

His two shrinks gave him drugs for it. The guy hallucinated. They gave him drugs! That's not thinking real well.

For me, when you start hallucinating, you stop taking drugs. That's what we did in the '60s. "See too many things that aren't there, lay off the drugs for a while." That's a good rule of thumb.

His shrinks also believed that his disorder was bad. I didn't. Dollar signs filled my eyes. I said to him, "This is a multi-million-dollar disorder!" The guy looked at me and said, "What are you talking about?" I said, "Does the term 'Playboy Channel' mean anything to you?"

When I said that, the clouds of schizophrenia parted in front of him. And when I said, "You never have to be alone again!" a smile spread from ear to ear. I said, "Think about it. We could run courses and train traveling salesmen in this. They could be monogamous and have the best time they ever had. This is a multi-million-dollar disorder that would give people the ability to never be lonely again."

I told him, "I want to know how to do this." And this guy, who had spent five years trying to get rid of a problem, began by saying, "Well, maybe I'll tell you and maybe I won't." Now that shows a changed attitude.

That shift stands behind a lot of what I do. Anything the brain can do will have a different value in another context. You have to understand—the brain does it! What may be a problem in one situation is success in another.

Slow Trancing and Fast Trancing

Most of you have experienced not having enough time, haven't you? Think about it. Don't the experiences you enjoy end too quickly? How come the ladies always smile when I say that? Most of you have also wanted some things to go faster, like waiting in line.

Most people have these things reversed. You wait in line to get into a play or movie that you're dying to see. You look at your watch and it says 8:00. The program starts at 8:15. You stand there and wait. Then you look at your watch; 8:00 and two seconds. Things you really enjoy go by faster than a snap of my fingers.

One day I sat around thinking about this. I realized, "*Your brain* does it!" All we have to do is go in and change this stuff around.

Now we'll do a very important piece of elicitation. This is your chance to make the things you enjoy last a hundred times longer, and make the things you don't enjoy get done quickly.

Just this morning the taxicab driver said to me, "We're going to be stuck in traffic; I know it's a bother; I know you're going to feel bad." I said, "And I know you're wrong." I just sat back and went into trance. I was here in two minutes. I looked at my watch and thirty-five had actually gone by. He was frazzled to the hilt; I felt wonderful.

I want things I enjoy to seem to last a lot longer. Eric Robbie and I have developed a way to do this together. When we teach workshops, we make the nights take forever. We got carried away with it in San Diego. The workshop ended at five. We went out for dinner and drinks. Finally, we looked at each other and said, "God, it must be getting really late. Maybe we should get some sleep for tomorrow." We looked at out watches and it was only 6:35. I call that having all the time you need.

Submodalities of Time

First, identify the submodalities of *fast time* and *slow time*. Do the same kind of eliciting as before. Do it faster. Skip the yakking in between. Be thorough. Go down the list of submodalities quickly and elicit *fast time* and *slow time*.

Second, be sure that *the person is in state*. Part of eliciting information involves being able to get people to access the state. That means being congruent.

Someone whimpered, "Well, I asked people to think of a really powerful resource. They just couldn't think of one." And I whimpered back "Well, you must have had one." But that doesn't make you want to think of one, does it? You could sneer, "You must have been happy sometime." Then they won't think so. Be congruent.

Third, evoke the state using all of your NLP tools. Since you have to get people really into the state where they can access it, use your tone, your tempo, and your voice. Also, mention instances, when you know, that time, has crawled, just, really... really... crawled...

Fourth, elicit pleasant experiences. It's especially important to find pleasant slow time. Have a preference for pleasant things. You want a time where time went slow, not slow bad, but slow good. All of us have had days that are just wonderful, and that seemed to last a year—like the first day of vacation. Sometimes if you work all year and then you go on vacation, the first day goes on forever while you do a million things.

I used to vacation in Tahiti a lot. I'd leave the rat race in California. I'd get on the plane and *rrrhhhhrr...* get a little jet lag going, and when I got to Tahiti, I'd do everything you could do in the first day. The natives seemed to move in slow motion while I was going *zzooom!*It took a while for me to slow down. I always loved that first day. I could do so much. I'd get up, play tennis, go diving, everything you could do, go swimming, go fishing, look at my watch, nine o'clock in the morning.

That's an example of time moving very slowly when I'm moving quickly. I like having lots of time to do things. I have a lot of fun and plenty of time to do more.

Fifth, juxtapose your time elicitations. Find an experience when time went *juuuuusssss* and was gone. The person will be able to make a comparison. Have the person really get back into it. You want him to notice the difference between when time moves quickly, and when it moves slowly.

Sixth, identify the specific submodality differences. Do they associate or dissociate? Does it position differently in the person's mind?

You will find some unusual aspects to this. It won't match the usual submodalities. With time distortion you may also have differences between various parts of the images. Sometimes the center of the images will be moving quickly, while other parts will be moving slowly. Maybe the sides of the images will be moving fast. It's a funny phenomenon. When you're blowing down the freeway really fast and you pull off into a forty-mile-an-hour zone, you feel like you're crawling. Do you know what I'm talking about? If you go from a twenty zone into forty-five you feel like you're going fast.

All of these things are "just in your mind." That's exactly where I want things. So I made that one of my favorite phrases.

Once I had a client who had paralysis in his leg. He said, "My psychiatrist says it's all in my mind." I said, "I don't think so. It looks like it's in your leg." The guy looked at me and said, "You don't think so?" I said, "Yes. In fact, it's in the other one now." He said, "You're right!" I said, "And it's gone in this one." He said, "It moves!" I said, "Yes it does. Now let's move it to your fingernails. Paralyze them now."

He could then walk, but his fingernails became paralyzed. It's not quite so limiting. He complained about his fingernails bitterly for years. I don't know about you, but my fingernails don't move around much. His wife told me that every time he would sit down he'd say, "These damned fingernails!" Maybe that's the secondary gain he got; he was in the habit of complaining.

Seventh, stack realities. In order to get a person into the state that gets the best elicitation, we add another dimension. Do you notice how I go about stacking things together? How I use quotes, metaphors, etc.?

Eighth, identify the person's timeline. As you do this elicitation, have the person give you a piece of information about time. In order to know how this person organizes time, we have to know the difference between his past and his future.

Stop right now and think about something that happened six weeks ago. See what you saw at the time; hear what you heard. Point to it. Where is it in your mind? Now think of something that happened six months ago. Point to that; all right. Now two years ago... three years ago. Go back to eight, ten years ago. Now, with your finger, draw a line through these representations and bring it up to the present.

Then pick something you know you will be doing in thirty days, like paying your rent. Then think of something you know you are going to do a year from now; then, something you are thinking about doing in two or three years. Continue using your finger to create your timeline.

You have a choice. Some people have the past in the back and the future in the front. Some people have the future in the back and the past in the front. Some people have it from right to left. You can use each in its appropriate occasions.

Ninth, use the timeline. Regardless of how the person's timeline is configured, have him literally see his timeline in front of him. Have the person turn physically while you're doing the elicitation. Then have the person stand up, turn, and literally back up to the last time he can remember being in exquisitely slow time. Check out what it looks like so you can refresh his memory.

Then have the person back up to a time when he did fast time. The reason for this is that, as his future disappears in front of him, he can literally pull the events that are now around him back up. The person can pull those events up until he is fully in the event. Then you can say, "Take a moment and relive fully this event; enjoy the process while you notice all the distinctions."

When the person has done that, have him put his timeline back where it was. Then you can do the conscious elicitation to find out the difference between slow time and fast time. When you get through this, I'm going to teach you a great way to do time distortion and put it to some fun results—things you can do with your family, friends, and business associates for fun and money.

Do Whatever Works

"Do they have to literally back up?"

Yes. Just have people turn and then have them pull it around them. They don't have to walk. Well, some people actually have to step backwards; you know, the *kinos,* they always have to do that. But people like that always do things more thoroughly than the rest of us. Others say, "Well, I thought about it, so it's kind of like I did it." *Kinos* have to get in there and actually feel it and enjoy it. If they have to walk backwards, that's fine. Remember, the rule of thumb, "Do whatever works!"

That rule can lead to a Renaissance in human lives. It cures people of the "fudge factor" and the "finagle phenomenon." These are two rampant phenomena in psychology.

When I started out, we tried to model what effective clinicians did. We didn't just model the greats like Virginia Satir, Fritz Perls and Milton Erickson. We also modeled people who were not well known, like Feritz Climents.

Feritz was one of the most effective clinicians I ever met. He was a Ph.D. in psychology who batted about .800. He just had a private practice and didn't make a big deal out of it. He didn't have any theories. I asked, "How do you know what to do?" He replied, "I don't know; it just comes to me." I said, "Where did you learn to do it?" He answered, "I don't know; I don't go to workshops or anything." I think he isolated himself so much he didn't know how to be stuck. He didn't have a theory so he wasn't stuck in anything. He did some amazing things.

What Won't Work

Theory doesn't work. People work, or not. When Gestalt, group therapy, T.A., or any other approach did work, it used different dynamics. Otherwise Gestalt psychologists could have trained other people to get the kind of results that Fritz could get. It wasn't the theory that worked, but the person. The part that worked lay in what the person did, not theory. When I worked with Virginia, I wanted to find out what made the difference in what she did that worked. I wanted to distill it so that what worked could be taught.

At that time I thought clients got blamed too much. I heard stuff like, "This client isn't ready to change." I heard things like, "Well, he's not mature enough. He's not responsible enough." As if the technique worked anyway! In physics we call this the "fudge factor." This applies where the technique is perfect, the theory is sound, but the result is obstinate.

Technically speaking, finagle phenomena generate the fudge factor. These are the often well-known but always unobservable events and structures which protect our pristine understandings from the intrusions of any reality. That's why we were always right.

This concept of "resistance" presupposes that a client can resist. Ludicrous. The idea that people are not ready to change is also ludicrous. If they're not ready to change, stop wasting their time and stop charging them! Have them come back when they get ready. What do you have to do? Monitor them until they get ready? Make them ready. If they need more time, take them into time distortion and give them the time.

The Joy of Challenge

In effective clinicians, like Milton, I found a different attitude. They looked at whatever got in their way as "This is where the fun begins." Milton's attitude in the face of difficulty was, "Ah! This is a rare opportunity to learn something new!"

Easy things don't stay fun. Working on an assembly line can get easy. Dealing with phobics, for instance, lost the fun for me. I teach other people to do that. What's fun for me is a client's situation that I have no idea how to fix.

When they brought Andy, the schizophrenic, to me, I had no idea what to do. To begin with, I had never heard of his situation before. Also, I wanted it before I fixed it. I wanted to be able to do it. Of course, I didn't want Mary from *Little House on the Prairie*. I had some of my own big-time fantasies. Pictures flew through my mind like crazy.

With Andy, I first started going through everything I know about changing images. I finally used what I call the "Bugs

Bunny cure." Have you ever seen the Bugs Bunny cartoon where the artist's pencil comes in and erases Bugs' tail? Then it erases his mouth so he can't talk. We did that. I gave Andy an erasing pencil. All I had to do was put one on the TV and have him pop the pencil out. Then he could begin erasing Mary's mouth and make her shut up.

This stands on a premise. When you accept the person's reality, everything becomes simple. The more their reality challenges you, the more exciting and satisfying they make your work.

Last Time Instructions

Tenth, distill your information. You will do this time-elicitation twice. First, you will send the person back in his timeline as you get him into state. Then you bring the person back. Have people go back and find their "slow time" to help refresh their memories. Bring them all the way back out and get the submodality information distinctions.

Then put them all the way back in and have them find a time where they had "fast time." Then bring them all the way back to consciousness to distill that submodality information.

Eleventh, do a contrastive analysis. Have your clients compare "slow time" with "fast time" by going through the contrasts, submodality by submodality. Check for any differences between the edges of images, in the centers, where their vision focuses, or where their consciousness lies.

Twelfth, anchor both experiences. Pay especially close attention here. You get to be a little bit tricky. Your clients do "slow time." You discover a difference in one submodality. Accentuate that difference and get an anchor for it. Reiterate that anchor for every difference you discover.

Get an anchor on one knee for "fast time" and another on the other knee for "slow time." By the time you have finished the elicitation, you will have two very powerful anchors. At that point, stop and come back here. Now I'm going to demonstrate how to use this.

Group Trance Induction

Your unconscious already knows about slowing down and speeding up time, and you have a rare opportunity as you leave here. I'd like your unconscious to realize that one of the things it can do is take a few minutes right now to close your eyes and deliberately go back and remember the things we did today. Take yourself back all the way to the beginning of the day.

I've learned that one reason people have trouble remembering to use skills and to take learning and understanding with them is that they don't go through an *encoding process*—putting a little cap on at the end of the day.

So go back to where we started, with non-verbal inductions and the handshake-interrupt, to how we used it and to every step we made today. Now take time to remember the things you went through; things that stood out as most important, the learnings, the understanding of generative systems—the things of value. Scan through them quickly in your mind.

Put it in fast time so you can run through as many things as you want to, as quickly as you want to, and still have time to relax in a growing comfortable state and to realize that what you're doing is a habit you can acquire. You can learn to take your own special learning anywhere you go.

One way to start is by beginning to put caps on segments of your experience so you remember to use these skills. The learnings you got here have no value unless you take them into your personal lives so you can, and will, learn both consciously and unconsciously. Consider the times and places where having control over time, of being able, to slow, time, way... down... would, be, of great help.

Stop and look into your slow time frame and put into it some of the things you would really like to have the time to enjoy—the things for which you want time to practically stand still—a certain flavor of food, that first feeling as your body hits the sheets, perhaps something you do—extra specially and intensely.

You also will be able to make time fly by for things that you want to go by quickly. Perhaps it's the traffic as you leave here. Anything that's a chore for you will go by quickly and still be pleasant. Learning to have control over your life is, as far as I'm concerned, what this is all about. It's learning to drive your own bus, to take your random subjective experiences and harness them, so they work for you in the most beneficial ways.

I will see you back here bright-eyed and bushy-minded at 10 o'clock tomorrow morning. You might find yourself having bizarre and pleasant and unusual dreams tonight. But you'll still wake up alert and ready to learn. I'll see you tomorrow morning.

VII

Slow Time Patterns
Questions and Answers

Today, we do more time distortion, to let these learnings settle in even more. By the way, I suggest that people start at the top of their clients' heads. Then talk about a person's forehead relaxing, and the muscles around their eyes.

We tried an experiment once with a friend of mine who owns a beauty school and teaches people to do facials. We took some people who were set for facelifts. We age-regressed them back to five years old. Have you ever noticed that when you age-regress someone they not only act younger but look younger? As we age-regressed these people we told them that their skin would stay five years old while their minds returned to their present ages. No one could find any value in that, could they?

Pop Submodalities

Do you have any questions?

"When I try to elicit submodalities from people, they often don't seem to know what I'm asking for."

When I go to NLP conferences, half the time I can't understand what people talk about. And I made it up! People coin all these new words. I stuck them in the Glossary. I use words, ideas, and experiences that people already know.

Computers usually come with a listing program. When you turn on the computer it can give you a menu. It lists letters with choices: pressing 'A' will give you this function; 'B' gives you another; press 'C' if you want something else. This simplifies things. You just point to the item you want.

I find this approach useful because lots of clients don't have much background or education. Some just have a lot of money. So instead of talking about submodalities, I use familiar words.

Ask, "Has your television ever gone on the fritz?" People say, "Yeah." So I say, "When you don't have a clear picture, you fiddle with different knobs that make the picture flip over, hold the horizontal, or change the brightness. You can tune the set with them. The better you tune it in, the more you can enjoy it." I then say, "Stop and think about the last time you had an absolutely exquisite time. You really enjoyed yourself. Now see it in your mind. See what you saw when you were there; hear what you heard. Now, slowly turn the brightness up."

If the person asks "How?" and scrunches up his face, or says, "I can't turn it up." I look at him real seriously and say "Underneath your picture there's a little panel. Can you see it now?" They say, "Yeah!" So I say, "There's a knob that says 'brightness.' Turn it up!" And they go, "Oooohh!"

I can't explain how this works. As a modeler, you don't have to know why things work. You just have to notice which things work and which things don't. This frees you from having to play theorist. In my case that brings great relief. I have minimal patience with theories.

Have people literally fuss with the focus. With the advent of video cameras and VCRs, a lot of people live on either end of those things. I do a lot of work with the Japanese consulate in San Francisco. With those guys, relate everything to cameras and VCRs. In this workshop, I'm looking at all your faces. The last time I did a seminar for the Japanese consulate, I didn't see a single face. I saw two hundred video cameras aimed at me. I said, "Turn up the brightness." They did it on their cameras!

Begin with simpler submodalities. You can relate submodalities more easily. Say, "Think of something pleasant; now turn the brightness up and notice how it intensifies your feelings. Now turn it way down. And then way up." This helps you to establish a reference point before you start eliciting.

Then pick two really dramatic things, like beliefs. Pick two that they believe strongly and yet don't really care about, emotionally, one way or the other. Notice if the pictures take different positions.

Covert Submodality Elicitation

Let me tell you one of my secrets. Before I ask about submodalities, I watch to see what the subjects do on the outside. Before I have them go inside and start thinking about it, I want to know half the answers. That way I can help them get into it.

If I say, "Now, I want you to think of something that you totally believe is true. Something like, 'Do you believe the sun is coming up tomorrow?'"I do not let them go and pick the strong belief. I select the reference for them to get.

People have a tendency to pick emotionally charged issues. Whenever people pick an emotional issue, they tend to get caught in it. That makes submodalities harder to do. The minute they see it, they start sniffling and going back into it. Not useful. Pick something with no emotional charge. You get higher quality information more easily.

Do your elicitation first. Then have them pick things they believe about themselves that they wished they didn't. A lot of my work is like this. Limiting beliefs get in the way of people doing successful trance phenomena or being successful in life.

Successful Beliefs

I do a success seminar with a guy named Robert Allen. He runs a program called Challenge Systems. He does a week-long program that changes a person's whole attitude about success.

His program induces people into a state of wanting to make money. First, he teaches people how to make money with real estate. He has buses that take people to banks and other places to get people out doing things. Then he lets them use his credit line to borrow money to do it with. He gets people into buying and selling real estate. He hammers them until they get on the highway and start doing things themselves.

In Robert Allen's book, *The Challenge*, he talks about going to the unemployment office. He walked around and picked three people at random who were just totally down on their luck. He took them and made them millionaires in one year, to prove he could do it. Now that shows guts! To prove a course works, get out and do it.

Robert and I decided we would do a success-oriented seminar. We would find the major beliefs that got in the way of people getting out on the highway and doing the best they could. A lot of people spent time looking for what could go wrong. Part of the problem is this negative orientation. Are you aware of that tendency in people who can't get with it?

You find it especially among people with a scientific background. Scientific method orients people negatively. The process involves making a hypothesis and trying to tear it apart. You look for what could possibly be wrong with it!

Negative orientation stinks if you want innovations. It really stinks for running your life. If you always look for what doesn't work—you find it. If you devote all your energies only towards looking for what could go wrong—that creates it.

People call this a self-fulfilling prophecy. Sometimes it's even simpler than that. Some things could go wrong. Some things could work. You find both out there. If you look through things that can go wrong, you find them. You just looked in the wrong pile. Look for what works—you'll find that as well!

Have you noticed that I almost always focus on pleasant things when I do elicitations? Along with that kind of elicitation, I may also realign people. So I ask them about something really pleasant.

Ask about a belief like, "The sun is going to come up." I never go for something questionable. That's too shifting. I'm not interested in what people doubt. I'm going to fix that anyway. With regard to something that might or might not be—who cares?

Submodality Accessing Cues

I begin by saying, "Think of one; now think of the other." When you do that, you get non-verbal responses; people say, "Yeah," and they turn to one side. "Now think of the other." And they say, "Okay" as they turn to the other side. Notice the subtle cue there! Remember the partners you worked with yesterday. It's that exaggerated, isn't it? People do this, they move their whole body right or left.

If you get caught up in looking at accessing cues, it doesn't help you to squint. I know some of you learned accessing cues, and the world became a giant Fellini movie for two months. You went into the supermarket and watched people with their eyes rolling like they belonged in pinball machines. "Hmmm, let's see, what shall we have for dinner? Well, I don't know. I tell myself... but it feels like I want this. But that doesn't look like it's a healthy enough meal. Pretty soon you have 300 people doing that, and pretty soon you're going, "DUH-duh, DUH-duh, just when they thought it was safe to go to the supermarket!"

Once I've detected a few accessing cues, it all becomes clear. You can tell the ones who do distance by watching how they focus they eyes. They either focus their eyes up out here or straight ahead. If you notice the difference, you can start seeing more.

Then the question becomes, "Do you also hear any sound?" When people move right, and then move left, it kind of gives away where they put things, doesn't it? Once you've noticed some of these more subtle cues, you realize they are not really that subtle. It's just that you haven't been looking for them.

People once thought accessing cues were subtle. Twenty-five years ago, when we pointed this out, people said, "This is ingenious! How did you notice it?" I said, "Well, we sit on a stage and ask people questions. When you ask an audience, 'Make a picture of a giraffe with a rhinoceros head,' and 300 people move their eyes up and to the left, you notice."

Guidelines for Eliciting

Psychologists always claimed they observed. They did talk about it; they didn't do it. They stayed busy putting interpretations on things. "If you cross your legs, you are closed. If you look away you lied." Stuff like that. How many of you got that crap?

Fritz Perls used to do that. Anytime anybody made a picture he'd shout, "Vat are you avoiding?" And the person would go, "Ahhhhh!" And Fritz anchored it. Then Fritz would say, "I want you to do this," firing the anchor. People did what he told them because he scared them. Fritz mastered scaring the shit out of people. The KGB could have built a model out of that.

Actually, you can elicit easily with naive subjects. They don't know to put any interpretation on it. I say, "Look, just to prepare..."

Use the word "just." Use it when you hear them say it too. Whenever you hear "just" from someone, you know you can reach the edge of their model. When you hear "just" or "because," your ears should lift up like radar. It means you grazed the edge and that you're ricocheting off just what they need to know. Mark that to yourself. You can always use anchoring to bring that back.

When you say, "just preparation," that implies, "We haven't begun yet." You haven't crossed the border from casual conversation into working and getting results yet. That puts your clients at ease. Just can also mean not important. If they worry, "I don't know if I'm doing this right." You say, "Don't worry, this is just preparation." Then they go, "Ahhh, okay. Well, the picture is over here, and the other one is over here, and it's this big, and this close, and the voice comes from over there." That helps you with elicitation.

Don't act like it's a big deal. Since I travel a lot, I often sit down on a bench or a bus or plane and begin talking. I'll say, "You know when you have to stop and you're getting impatient and you make those pictures in your head?" And people say, "Yeah, the ones up here." You see, they don't know they're not supposed to talk about this. Instead of making it sound pseudo-scientific, act like everybody does it. Everybody does do it.

I find that I get the cleanest easiest information before we "really" begin a session. I use a technique called "shooting the bull" with my clients. I come in and say, "It's a nice day." I talk about something. Really, I go through a listing program. I begin when I told you to begin, long before the start. Usually I officially begin after we've already finished.

If you say, "Okay, let's start now," they may go blank! You have to edge your way in. Put them at ease. I tell jokes to get clients loosened up. Anchor them so you can keep their humor available.

I also give them lots of examples so they can answer the questions. I say, "Well, for me beliefs go over here." Actually it's not my programs I'm talking about; it's what I saw in *them*. When I see they have theirs sorted side to side, I'll describe how I do it, only I'll describe theirs. It will sound familiar to them. They'll go, "Ahhh! I do the same thing!" It puts them further at ease, and lets them know they can get the information.

Real Limits

Whenever I reach a limit of what people can do, I set up finger signals with them and then ask their unconscious if they have reasons why they couldn't. You can use any unconscious signal.

I ask if they can make adjustments, at the unconscious level, to allow them to do this for just this length of time. You can use the six-step reframing model.

As a general principle, whenever you have a difficult trance phenomenon, it usually intersects with your reality strategy. All of us have ways of telling the difference between real and not real. This is why we are capable of walking through a door instead of banging into the wall. If you picture a door where there isn't one, and you don't have the ability to tell which is the picture and which is the door, you're going to bang into the wall a lot.

Most of us, as we grow up, develop such abilities. How many of you had imaginary playmates when you were children? It's all right. Everybody does it to some extent. How many imaginary pets? When you're a child that's fine. When you grow up people start hammering you not to have these. You don't want to be talking to imaginary people in public. Some real people will lock you up! Do it privately and have fun.

Just like Andy, the schizophrenic I spoke of earlier, people often become scared when you do trance work. Have you had that experience? You start to do something and your heart goes "Ahhhh!" That's because you have come up against your reality strategy. It's a significant signal. Pay attention.

When that happens, back up a step and build in safeguards. Orient your clients so their unconscious will only do it for five minutes. Or say, "The image will glow funny and have a label saying 'hallucination.'" Do something that adheres so you don't end up with no way to know the differences between something that's there and something that's not.

Set up finger signals to be a client yourself. Let the unconscious do the work. Say, "Look, I want to be able to do trance work with this person. Would it be all right? Will you make the necessary adjustments at the unconscious level to allow this person to do it just this once? If they start to do anything that may be harmful, pop me right out of trance."

You'll be surprised how often you will get a yes signal from the unconscious. If you get a no signal, go in and start negotiating. This book's appendix has a seven-step model that shows you how to negotiate with the unconscious. It's the same model you use with the conscious mind, but it's simpler. With conscious minds, you have to use reframing. You have to say, "It'll be okay!" The book *Reframing* will tell you more than you want to know about this.

Conscious minds need to be reassured. The unconscious processes just need ways that work to get things done. That's how they function.

Teasing, Mixed-State Communication and Complaining

"What do you do with professional complainers who say they have never had anything positive?"

You know they're lying. Tease them. That's what I do; I tease them... into it. It depends on what it is. But I'm sneaky. I don't let them start complaining.

I kid complainers so much that I start out with a pleasurable experience. Then when they begin complaining I say, "You were laughing a few minutes ago." Then they sigh, "Well, yes, but I wasn't *really* enjoying myself." So I commiserate, "Well, that's probably all you can do. So go back and pick some other experience that was a lot of fun but you didn't *really* enjoy."

When complainers dissociate from pleasant memories, they say things like that. Get a good dissociated image. Have them make it bigger and brighter until it's glowing. Have them walk around back and step in. Then say, "This will do; it's not *real* pleasure, but it's just enough enjoyment. It's the best you can do, unless your unconscious can double it, now!" Then you start amplifying it that way.

With whiners and moaners you always have to come in the back door. But that can be cured.

I like using the tongue-tied induction to cure people of chronic complaining. I first use a technique called "mixed-state communication." It's a way of getting trance phenomena without really going through trance work. Basically, you focus your eyes about two inches behind their eyes. Then, as you ignore the person's conscious mind, talk straight to his unconscious. One does not have to be in trance for unconscious processes to be effective.

As you look beyond the eyes, start complimenting the person's unconscious processes. "You, Joe's unconscious mind, must be really frustrated with the way he treats you. He doesn't give you the respect you need. And I think it's about time that you demonstrated your power to him. Do you understand that and agree with that now?"

You'll get the head nodding. The person will also feel it as it happens.

Lots of people try to act like the conscious mind plays the whole game. It can't. Consciousness is a focus of awareness used to function from event to event. The unconscious processes play nearly all of the game, and they have the rule book.

You have all these pictures in your head, don't you? Where do they go when they go away? What about all the ones that you don't notice now?

I hear, "They're stored chemically." You bet! In some people, real chemically. You know who you are! You laughed and went, "Mmmmmm... not me."

Once you've set the stage say, "In order to demonstrate your power and your effectiveness, so you can unify your unconscious and your conscious resources, I think it's time that you showed him that you can do something. For example, you know how you sometimes get tongue-tied, where a word is there and you can't quite make it come out? You know what that is. I want you to do that every time he starts to complain."

Of course, that's a come-on. People will try to complain. They'll go, "Ahhh, ahhh..." pausing, trying to speak, stuttering. You can say, "That's right!" They always go, "Woooowww!"

I had a shrink, Bob Shawls from Berkeley, who runs a Gestalt Institute. His wife, a Ph.D. psychologist, got into NLP. He, eventually, became a NLPer.

She brought him in because they argued about whether NLP was real. They came in and sat down and I listened to them argue. Now, I have no patience with people arguing. So I turned to them and I yelled, "Shut up!" Then I said, "Look, if you're arguing about whether NLP is real or not, I can solve that for you. It's not! I made it up. It's a drug experience. Think of it that way. Just don't argue anymore."

They said, "Well, we argue about other things." I said, "I thought so. But aren't you married?" They said, "We are." I asked, "Is this *why* you got married? So you could argue? Is that what you were thinking about at the time?" Then I looked at him. I said, "When you first decided you wanted to spend your life with your wife, what was on your mind then?"

Talk about something worth anchoring! Chheeeesssshhhh! Because I wanted that glow in his face, I anchored it. Then, every time she started to bring up a subject, I fired off the anchor. He'd look at her with that look of passion. That will re-anchor the crap out of a relationship. I like that maneuver.

As I did this, the husband kept saying, "I know you're anchoring me and it's not working." And she kept saying "It is working! It is working!" I know, I love to torture them. It's fun.

Finally, I turned around and looked past the guy's eyes the same way and I said, "You know, I know he's a psychiatrist. But I know *you've* been driving the bus for years. You keep his heart beating; you keep his blood pressure steady; you let him know where he's going in the morning; you can now make his hand shake automatically. But he doesn't appreciate you! Isn't that a slap in the face?"

The guy's hand rose; first he slapped his right cheek and then his left. Baammm! He said, "God, I'm so impressed!" It wasn't about lost control. He was such a control freak that he couldn't have some kinds of experiences he wanted.

You can skip the mystery. Sometimes you can remember somebody's name and sometimes you can't. Your conscious mind doesn't drive the bus. It doesn't need to. It's too much work.

Human Potential Response

In the human-potential movement some things rot my socks. Some people keep acting like being authentic means not being responsive.

Maslow set the direction. Abraham Maslow was the visionary of humanistic psychology, Carl Rogers was the saint, and Fritz

Perls was the superstar. I see it that way. Maslow described the authentic man as, of course, himself! That meant being aloof and reading a lot. He was a college professor.

Authentic, for Maslow, meant to so completely control your own feelings that people couldn't make you feel things. I proposed a $5000 bet. I said, "I bet anybody $5000 that, if they stay in a room with me for ten minutes, I can make them feel things, without touching them."

I had takers! Some people in the human-potential movement actually believed that drivel so much that they put their money where their mouths were. So they'd walk into the room. Before they sat down I'd shout, "F—k you!" They'd go, "Bhhhhhh!" And I'd say, "Made you feel something! Give me the money!"

Of course, giving someone "the finger" is an anchor too. In Germany they point to the side of their heads and make circles around their ear with their finger. The gesture means "you have a bird in your head." You're disorganized; the biggest insult for Germans. To insult Americans, tell them to go have sex. I never understood that one. I can understand, as an insult, telling someone to eat shit. Telling someone to go out and have a good time just didn't seem like an insult.

The processes we deal with here occur at unconscious levels. Your ability to respond makes the difference between you and furniture. Those people at Esalen tried to deep trance identify with furniture. You can respond. That makes you human and authentic. Human means that somebody of the appropriate sex can look at you in a certain way that starts the juices rolling.

Choosing Response Ability

Realize, beyond the question of just responding, what response you generate, and how you generate it. Often you dislike the way you respond, or that others respond to you. You may dislike it when you get too angry with your children. You may dislike the fact that your husband scrapes his toes. Maybe you pulled your hair out! The problem isn't *that* you respond, it's *how* you respond. Being able to change from one response to another gives you the keys to control and authenticity.

I once worked with an organization that did some big things with couples counseling. But they tried to reduce it all to sexuality and things from a person's childhood. For me, it boils down to this: if you live with someone long enough you get some *bad anchors*. This guy scrapes his toes or leaves his clothes on the floor. She walks in and sees. She goes through the ceiling! Bad anchor!

Good reframing takes care of bad anchors. Induce a different feeling in them and attach it to the clothes. Look at them and ask them to think of a when they felt "the *most lonely* you've ever been." Then anchor it. Say, "I know there are thousands and thousands of women out there who are so *alone*. They feel this way." Fire the anchor. "Every time you see clothes on the floor you will know that you are not alone." If you can anchor the difference between feeling you have a companion and feeling totally lonely, that's all you need to do.

Of course, you could also get the guy to pick up his clothes. There's nothing that a trance can't fix. Make it so that when he throws them down his hand will know it. Use the "shoplifting technique." When his hand goes out it slaps both sides of his own face.

I did a project in Philadelphia on shoplifting. We ran a big ad campaign against it. I worked for an ad agency that wanted to see if we could affect this on a mass basis. We put up billboards all over town and bought ten-second radio ads as well as TV time. On television we put one sentence across a white screen. It said, "Shoplifting is stealing." Nothing else. We hammered the city with it day and night. Shoplifting in that city dropped by 22 percent. If people don't think of shoplifting as stealing, they do it. They know stealing is bad.

When you change the way people think and feel about things, they act differently. A guy, tired, comes home. He throws his clothes on the floor. That's one thing. If he goes to throw his clothes down and it makes him feel bad, he won't do it. If you yell at him, he will just avoid you and throw his clothes down when you're not there! Attach the bad feelings to the clothes—you don't want them attached to you. Have the clothes make him feel bad when he throws them down.

Think about how you train a dog. When the dog goes to the bathroom, you don't make him feel afraid of you so he hides in the corner and shits. You can make him afraid of having his nose shoved in it. He learns, "If it's outside, it's good. If it's inside, it's bad." Same with cats; you give them a litter box. Then you start sliding it toward the door. Eventually you put it on the front porch. Then you take it and move it out in the yard.

The Art of Accurate Anchors

"What do you do if you anchor and you don't get a strong response?"

Anchors never work the same. But your unconscious can sort anchors. With audiences I use visual anchors. The most important thing for you to learn is to anchor the same thing in the same place. You can remember it.

Anchors are never identical. Anchoring depends on where they touch you and how fast. Part of anchoring depends on who you do it with, the tone of your voice, the subject you talk about, and the rate of speed at which you talk.

Generally, the more precise you make an anchor, the more impact it will have. Anchor as precisely as you can. If you had trouble establishing really powerful anchors, try putting some chalk on your fingertips. This will help you be precise when you touch your client. Then, when you have a good anchor, you can fire it off and get an intense response.

Sometimes responses lack the intensity of what you elicited. Use the magic technique of chalk. Anchor somebody with chalk on your fingers so that you get marks. When you go back to fire the anchor you can anchor it in *exactly* the same spot.

Remember, anchors depend on more than location. Anchoring works in all modalities. Use all the submodalities.

Anchor Demonstration

Think of something wonderful. Close you eyes and remember the last time you felt wonderful lust. Close your eyes and just remember. Now take your picture and make it bigger; make it brighter; intensify *this!* Now I've anchored. That's right.

Now I want you to think of one thing your mate does that annoys you. Let it be something that's not all that important; maybe she leaves something out all the time. Do you know what I mean?

"I can't think of anything."

There's nothing your mate does that bothers you? What a guy! Why don't I believe you? You can't be with another human being and have nothing... Boy, it popped right in there! It's just an intuition I had. I don't know why.

Now close your eyes on whatever it is. As you do I want you to feel *this!* That's right. You might not find it so annoying; it might become romantic. For me, you've got to take things that bother you and enjoy them. This is one of the nice things about being able to control subjectivity. Now we're ready for some trance work.

Your Own Time

Who needs more time in here? I want you to think of something that goes by too quickly, something that you would like to last a lot longer. Can you think of something like that? Why does this lady smirk? Come up here. Now keep it a secret. *Remember,* I'm not into divulging things.

Do you remember the lady yesterday who hallucinated something in her hand? Afterwards somebody came up and asked me what was in her hand. I have a problem with that. *She vas askink der wrong person.*

Contralateral Induction

First, I want you to take a deep breath so I can show another induction. Now do the same things I do. Okay? Focus your eyes right there, and watch what I do with my hands and arms in your peripheral vision.

Begin by putting your hands straight out in front of you. Now lift them over your head. As you lower them, take one arm and cup your hand nearer you while the other hand points straight out. As your arms go all the way down, begin to lift them up, and turn them to face each other so that they are open; let them both go up. Then reverse your hands so you're pointing with the other one. Now bring your arms down that way. Then lift both arms up like... hold them there and close your eyes right now. That's right.

Now let your arms go down only at the speed at which you begin to feel comfortable and relaxed and *go all the way down.* Deeper and deeper into a trance. Perhaps deeper than you have ever gone before. Very slowly now, so your hands are touching your thighs only when your *unconscious* is ready to *learn something of immense and wonderful value.* All the way down now. Deeper and deeper and deeper. That's right.

Time to Trance

What I want you to do, unconsciously of course, is to make preparations to feel yourself *let go...* deeper into a trance so you can float back on the wings of time and change, now. Way, way back.

I want you to get a little bit younger with each breath. A year at a time. Younger and younger. See a birthday or a pleasant event from each year as you *step back* in your mind, getting a little bit younger with each breath.

As you get younger, you will recapture your childlike ability to learn what's always been inside you—your ability to experience things. When you were very young a month seemed like forever. As you get older, months seem to just zip by. When you were very young, and it was five minutes before you got to go outside and play, five minutes were an eternity.

What your unconscious is doing now is remembering how to *feel things* the way it wants to. I know your unconscious remembers the work you did yesterday when this woman was an adult doing those experiments. And it knows the difference between slow time and fast time. Now I want you to make the preparations, at this age, so that in a moment, when I reach over and touch her on the arm like this, she's going to zip back to the event that she wants to last a lot longer and suddenly time will *s-l-o-w d-o-w-n*. It will almost stand still. As it does she will relive one of those events. In real time it will take two minutes, but it will *seem like an hour*. That's right.

When your unconscious is ready and has made all the necessary adjustments it can let me know by lifting this finger up... just like that, with honest unconscious movement. That's right.

I want your unconscious, now, to take all the time it needs to make these preparations. It is drifting deeper and deeper, making the unconscious adjustments to getting younger, so when she pops back to her present age she will be ready to experience something of great enjoyment and have it last so she can relish it and enjoy it. That's right. Going just deep enough to really enjoy that experience. All the way down now, deeper and deeper, making those adjustments at the unconscious level.

Now I want your unconscious to give me a full response. I'm going to reach over and move your arm all the way down so I can very clearly see that finger move when your unconscious is ready. That's right. There you go. Begin now. Really enjoy it—fully, completely. That's right. Really enjoying yourself now. As time flies by for you... you have one minute left.

Here we go. All the way up. One, two, three. Now. I want you to let that hand go down only at the rate at which every time you're in this experience, your unconscious is ready to experience it and no faster. Now. There you go. Say to yourself, "Yum!" Thank you.

Contralateral Explanation

Moving the arms up and down this way creates cerebral competition. The right and left hemispheres communicate with each other through the corpus callosum. This starts a lot of contrary messages going in opposite directions. The trick is starting out with the palms up. The purpose is to create rapid inductions.

It's like Milton Erickson's confusion technique. He would confuse someone and then take them into trance, since confusion is a doorway into new learning and altered realities. It's also like the handshake-interrupt. You catch people mid-program. This is a little different way of inducing an altered state.

Contralateral control means that the brain's right hemisphere controls the left side of the body, and the left hemisphere controls the right side. Each hemisphere can control its same side, isolateral control, to some degree. When you do the same thing at the same time with both sides of your body you use both contralateral and isolateral control from the dominant hemisphere. It tends to take over.

When you do several different things simultaneously with your body, one hemisphere can't handle it. You demand both hemispheres. Then you laterally reverse what you did. Both hemispheres compete for control of both sides of your body.

More, both of these gestures have hard programmed emotional associations. Those of you familiar with Virginia Satir's stress postures may already have known. That fires off a lot of other programs.

Do it palms up and very slowly, lifting the arms up together. You want to really get the deep kinesthetic programs running. So do them together. As they drop down, you point one and cup the other. Then turn them to face each other. Bring them up together. Then reverse it.

Look at me while you're doing this and you will feel it when it works. Something inside you will go "Bbbzzzzzzz."

Instructions for Slow Time

We just did an induction of time distortion. We also did something else you can use to really help yourself—regression. Age regression can help you with most hypnotic phenomena. When you were younger, you had a more flexible subjectivity. I like to use a juxtaposition of actual and what we call partial age regression. You don't age-regress people to the point where they forget being an adult. You age-regress only the parts that you want in order to recapture the flexibility of consciousness.

When you do this exercise with your partner, remember to use it to make pleasant things last longer. We'll do that first. Afterwards we'll get to make mundane things go by quicker. By now you should have a specific list of submodalities that make time go by very quickly and submodalities that make time go by very slowly for you.

Stack your suggestions so the person goes back because you remember when you were a kid how long time took? Do you remember that? It's just like the phenomenon of how big houses were then. If you remember the first two years you went to school... it seemed to take forever, didn't it?

You still have that subjective sense of time encoded in your memory. The subjective sense that some things seem to take forever—that is encoded within you. Now we want the things that are pleasant to take a long time.

So take people, age-regress them back, not fully but partially. So they have an adult's consciousness and a child's unconsciousness. Once you've age-regressed them back, have their unconscious put up all those submodalities of slow time on a screen. Then have the unconscious put the event the person wants to enjoy in the future on the screen so that it now seems to be taking a lot more time.

When your clients get to that point, have them step through those submodalities and be there. Always make a distinction

between real time and trance time. What will take only two minutes in real time will seem like it takes a half-hour to an hour in
trance time.

You will find any number of ways to do age regression. You
can also make it fancy. Trance encourages your verbal and imagi-
native artistry.

Milton used to do something else pretty creative. The first
time I saw him do it I had to leave the room because I started
laughing too hard. And Milton hated it when you laughed too
hard. He's a serious man you know.

Once he had a lady in a trance. He said, "And when you open
your eyes, you won't know who your are, but you will do everything I say." Then he said, "Okay, now open your eyes." He said,
"Hi." She asked, in a child's voice, "Who are you?" And he said,
"I'm the person who's going to give you the book of time."

He then picked up nothing and continued, "I want you to
take this book." She said, "Okay." Milton said, "Now, this is the
book of your life. You see yourself sitting in a chair on that page,
now." And she said, "Yeah!" He said, "Now with each page that
you turn back you will see one year earlier, and you'll be one year
younger. And I want you to turn that book back to where you are
honestly and completely five years old."

This lady sat there in trance doing this. Each time she
turned the page you could see her face change, and she started
looking more and more like a little kid. I started cracking up.
Milton looked at me; if his arm hadn't been paralyzed because he
wanted it to be right then, I'm sure he would have flipped me off.
We had a deal; I picked on him, but only when we were alone.

Concentrate on breathing at the same rate as the person. Concentrate on your tempo and on lowering your voice tone.

Set up some way to age-regress the person back. Set up finger signals again in that state.

Do it step-by-step, methodically. When I demonstrate I go through this very quickly. I've been doing it for a long time.

When you set up finger signals, ask the unconscious if it will set up the grid and make time go as slowly as it did when the person was a child. Then the person may pick one event to really enjoy and have it seem like it goes on for a long time. Set the grid up so you can do something that only takes five minutes but seems like it takes an hour.

Tell the person ahead of time that you're going to reach over and touch him on the shoulder, and that when you do, five minutes of clock time will go by, but it will seem like an hour. Ask the unconscious to get ready and make all the necessary adjustments to ensure and guarantee. Always use those kinds of words. Have it give you a yes signal so you know it's ready to begin.

When you get that yes signal, touch the person and say, "Begin now." Remember, people in trance are extremely literal. Get a watch and notice when their time's up. Otherwise, when they get to the end, they'll just keep going until something stops them. Give them a limit by saying things like, "One-fifth of the way there. Two-fifths of the way there..." It's the first time for them. Your marking time will help them start learning ways of adjusting for a subjective sense of time while in trance.

Applications of Time

Think of all the things you can do with this! Milton used to take musicians who didn't have time to practice and have them practice in trance. How about having your students practicing their skills while in trance? You can tell them to do it with implicit muscle movements so they develop dexterity and skill. You can give them hours of practice in trance time and it won't take that much real time. You can do tremendous things.

How many of you play golf? You can practice while you ride on the train. Tell your unconscious to sort out the feelings between the swings that are going to work and the ones that are not. Tell it to develop a little voice that says, "Yes!" and one that says, "No!" That way you can adjust your stance.

Professional golfers taught me this when I built a model from them. They constantly adjust their stance before taking the shot. They adjust, and then look up. For one golfer I modeled, the fairway shrunk; that told him to swing. If it didn't shrink, he wouldn't do it. He kept readjusting until his body went into the right position. Your intuitions always know, just before you hit the ball, whether you got it right or not. Get that intuition one step back so you don't actually swing until you have it right.

How to End the Trance

After you age-regress the person, set up the grid and get a commitment from the unconscious mind; then have the person run through something that ends too quickly, something the person can luxuriate in, and wants to take a long time. Give him that experience. Then bring him out. Switch it around and do it the other way so the person can experience time going by faster. Once you do that, we can move on to something else.

Also, when you bring people out of trance, give them the post-hypnotic suggestion that whenever time might fly by too quickly, and they want to relish and enjoy the experience more, the unconscious mind can kick this in automatically so that life is more of a party! Okay, go get yourself a partner.

Quick Contralateral Trance

I want you to take your palms and hold them up, and then look straight ahead. Pick a spot where there's reflected light and focus your eyes on it. Then put your hands higher and together. As you go down very slowly, separate your hands, cup one, and point one straight ahead. Then slowly bring them up together again and reverse them. Then down. Slowly bring them up; slowly bring them together.

Then let your eyelids close at the same rate at which you drop into a deep trance. Now. That's right… all the way down. Take a deep breath; relax and enjoy feeling yourself beginning to go into a deeper and deeper state, with the knowledge that you're about to learn how to use this. Take this feeling; it's a basis of learning and understanding that will stay with you for the rest of your life. And now return slowly back here to Earth Coincidence Center, remembering this feeling and enjoying it.

VIII

The Trance Phenomenon of Hyperesthesia:
Heightened Awareness

In the last chapter we dealt with the phenomenon of internal time distortion. Didn't that put you in a very altered state?

We all know some tasks that we want to perform where it would not be a good idea to be in *profoundly* altered states, like driving. We also want to learn to develop trance states less of profound alteration and more of heightened awareness.

People who listen to hypnosis tapes in their cars shouldn't drive. One guy actually hit a fire hydrant. He had some hypnosis tapes that we sold. Then he drove on the San Diego freeway, which is ten lanes wide, and where people drive wild. The tape said, "Now allow your eyes to close." He did. Then it said, "That's right." He turned right into a fire hydrant! Not what we want to do.

We have other altered states. These include states of *heightened perception*. So far we have dealt with the going-down trance. I now want to show you how to use the down trance to move people in the other direction. The really great trances induce what we call hyperesthesia—heightened awareness.

A lot of people have used trance work to create numbness. You get the unconscious to numb a person's arm and shove a pin through it. All well and good. I'd prefer that my body parts felt better than numb. I don't know if you can think of any uses for that, but something *might* come to mind. Ohhhhh, it's starting to ricochet off the back wall now. What could that be?

Double Induction Hyperesthesia

Would you two like to come up here?

I want to introduce you to double-induction technology. This makes hypnosis even more fun. You get to do it with a partner.

Double-induction technology helps you *deepen* trances very rapidly. That proves very useful when you want to use a trance to get more into the waking state. Learn more ways to use the submodalities from experiencing fast and slow time. Push those submodalities into the back of your minds so we can really open up perceptions. The world will become clearer. Things will move slowly. You will actually see more. Could that have value for you?

When I work with clients, I go into a profoundly altered state in which I have all the time I need to know what to do. I move a lot faster than my clients. I move faster than reality. Many times I actually hear the clients talking slowly. They seem to move slowly. This allows me to anchor and to watch their responses. At the same time I magnify the world so I can literally see the pores of someone's skin.

Remember, your brain can do this. It happens to you all the time, doesn't it? When you drive down the freeway, when you get off, the world goes into slow motion. Sometimes things look bigger. Or, when you go back home, and meet someone you used to know, he won't seem as big as he used to.

Double-induction technology will improve your sensory awareness. When doing NLP, some people squint. They have a client go back and remember something, and they look for responses by squinting. Or they try to get real close. That's *not* the way to do it.

First, amplify the responses in the people you work with. Then open your senses wide so that things get bigger. Instead of having to look closely to see changes in skin color, let your mind exaggerate them internally.

Remember, the things you see occur on your cortex anyway. You make things look closer, or in slow motion, in deep trance. You can also do it with your eyes open and your mind alert. You can actually have a far more alert state than you knew. You can make the colors brighter than you actually see them. It's a possibility, *now*.

Double Induction with Language Demonstration

With this lady's assistance, we'll show you this process twice. We'll use the same kinesthetic induction of cerebral competition. We'll also use a linguistic induction.

Our cerebral hemispheres process language differently, and preferentially process different parts of language. Since the hemispheres process language differently, we are going to put different parts of language into each ear. For a right-handed person, the person on the right side will speak to the left hemisphere. Reverse it for a left-handed person.

Many people say that the "dominant" hemisphere is logical and not intuitive. They say, "I'm trying to get into my right hemisphere to be intuitive." Bull!

The most intuitive thing you do is use language. You know, without knowing why, whether a sentence is well-formed or not. If I say, "Colorless green ideas sleep furiously," as opposed to, "Sleep furiously ideas colorless are," your brain goes "First sentence, syntax right; second sentence, syntax wrong." If I say, "Tom went to the store," your brain goes, "Well-formed sentence!" That all takes place in the left hemisphere, the one that isn't supposed to have intuition!

We know this because we have experimental results from people who actually tried it out. That makes the difference between a theory and a model. Actually, for most of you, the left hemisphere processes syntax. Syntax means all the rules about which ways to put words one after another.

We want to overload the left hemisphere. I'm going to use qualification predicates. That way we can build huge involved syntactic structures. "The more you try to stop yourself from preventing the fact that you're not able to fully understand yet, all the things that are beginning to continue to go on, inside your hemisphere they will soon become clearer than they ever did before, after I tell you each and every single thing that you need to hear, now."

Complex enough for you? I think you'll enjoy it. In double inductions you don't have to work so hard.

I'll induce trance by overloading the left hemisphere with qualification predicates and complex syntax. At the same time, we'll engage the right hemisphere. This non-dominant hemisphere has eidetic memory. It makes pictures in forms that recall all things that went before.

You could as well call the right the non-creative or non-intuitive hemisphere. Twits talk about the creative and non-creative hemisphere. They have their hemispheres mixed up, or split up.

The right hemisphere remembers nursery rhymes. "Mary had a little lamb, its fleece was white as..." or "A B C D E F..." Your brain has to finish that, right? That works on the right hemisphere. Say fragments of nursery rhymes and the songs that you remember as children. The more common the better. The less of it you say, so they recall the rest, the better. Tell people to see bits and pieces of buildings from their childhood.

The non-dominant hemisphere also uses the kinds of grammar that babies use, peda-grammar. Use baby talk, in baby tones. "Momma, bye-bye. Trance deep. Going now. In to." Use two-word utterances like these. "Laughing down, Eyes closed. Sleeping deep." Use that baby tonality when you do it. "Sleeping deeper. Trancing now."

Double Dual Induction Hyperesthesia

Then you put these elements together. Those of you in literature land can imagine the kinesthetic induction. Simultaneously, you can make up the childhood phrases and rhythms and pitch of my cohorts voice.

For this demonstration we'll to do it twice. The trick for you is to listen to either me or to John—one or the other, but not both. Or listen to both and let your unconscious…be…there now. Deeper go.

Once these two people are in trance, we will to demonstrate how to do hyperesthesia. That is, I'm going to make suggestions so they will develop heightened perceptions. When you do this you will remember what we do here. It will be clear and stay in your mind. Memory have; of this. Can remember. All things. See what; do now.

We're going to take your arms now. I want you to pick a point like that metal point on that pole. See how the light glistens off of that, comfortably. We are going to move your arms; I want you just to let them relax; we'll do the work for you. When we talk to you there's no need to understand consciously, for he'll do the work for you. You ready now?

As you begin to, you may not be hearing each and every thing but before you try to stop yourself all the way from holding, right there. That's right. All the way. Eyes close now, going deeper. As you listen to each and every relaxing word that you hear, you can and will go deeper, but before you try to stop yourself from preventing the fact that you're going all the way, deeper and deeper into a trance, your unconscious can and will learn to continue the process of going deeper and deeper, now. Into a trance, all the way down with growing comfort, more and more comfort and satisfaction.

Just allow yourself to go into a deep trance. All the way down. Deeper and deeper still. Take a deep breath and relax, really relax.

You can start to relax your forehead, because the more you stop yourself from preventing this the more you will continue deeper and deeper, because you're about to learn, now, really about going down with a growing sense of comfort. Because what we're about to do is enrich and increase your sensory experience so you can see the world more, hear the world more and feel the world more…all the way down now. That's right. All the way down, deeper and deeper still.

I want you to go back into your memory, now, and find some tranquil, pleasant past memory—a time when you were outside and enjoying yourself and the sun felt warm on your body and you enjoyed yourself. The sun seemed to be brighter; the leaves seemed more colorful. You seemed to have greater perception than you ever had before. That's right.

The more you go down deeper and deeper, the more I want your unconscious to prepare you for what you're about to do. Because as you drift down, I want your unconscious to find all the wiring and neurology at the unconscious level, so that later on when I reach over and touch you right here, your eyes will open and you will be more alert than you've ever been before.

But take all the time you need. Your unconscious will take you down to make these changes so that when you come out of this trance you will be more alert, more sensitive and more aware of your environment. Go down with comfort and a growing sense of satisfaction, and enjoy letting your unconscious do the work.

And now we have second subject. We'll begin with the kinesthetic induction again, moving arms up and down.

And now I want you to listen to each and every word I say, as
your eyes close and you begin to listen, really to listen to each and
every thing...because before we continue you can and will listen to
each and every word I say but not before you try to stop yourself
from preventing the fact that, as your hands begin to go down,
you're going to make adjustments at the unconscious level...to
make changes, powerful changes, such that the volume in your
ears increases intensely; such that your hearing, becomes so precise,
that sound, *moves, into, a sloow-motion*, state.

And I want your unconscious to allow your hands to go all the
way down only at the rate at which you make the necessary adjustments, at the unconscious level, to make colors brighter, the world
slower, and sounds richer and deeper and louder. That's right.

There you go. Take all the time you need to do that. Such
that when your hands go down and rest comfortably on your
thighs, you will have made the necessary adjustments, so that, the
world, will look, and sound, like it is, almost, in, slooww, mmotionnn...
That's right. Take all the time you need. And when I touch you
like this I will know you're ready to open your eyes and be more
alert than you have ever been before. That's right. And you'll see
things that will surprise you delightfully.

Because what each of you is doing right now is learning...
learning how to increase your perceptions and use your own natural neurology, so that in a moment when you're fully ready, I'll
know it. When I reach over and touch you appropriately, what
will happen is that you will come out of trance but your eyes will

be sped up, your hearing will be enriched and there will be a particular place right here on your body that will become so sensitive to touch that it will surprise you.

I want you to say the word "quicker" inside your head, the moment you open your eyes, so that when you want to go back into this state, you say "quicker" in just that way. It will allow you to turn on your perceptions at any moment you want, and give you the ability to take this feeling and put it anywhere in your body. You can tap that enriched state where you can feel more intensely, see more clearly; the colors get brighter, the world moves a little slower, and your hearing is much more profound.

So when I signal you, you will actually awaken, not only all the way out of a trance, but more out of a trance than you've been in years. That's right...making all the necessary adjustments. All the way up. Up, up right through the ceiling and out. When you open your eyes, I want you just to enjoy the perceptions and feel a little warmth here. Look around and notice how slow a blink can be. That's right. There you go.

Now, all the way up. Eyes opening, just enjoying the process. Look around and notice that you can look at the world in a way that enables you to see and hear things more profoundly than you have before. Smiles look bigger and brighter. Life's wonderful. Everything gets bigger. That's right.

Then just close your eyes and go all the way back down, way down. And tell yourself that any time you want to go back into that state you can and will by saying your own code word and enjoying the process, knowing you can feel good in all kinds of ways and places—if you catch my drift. That's right. And when you are ready and feel like you want to, allow your eyes to open. Come back into the waking state, or cheat if you want to. Thank you.

Double Induction Instructions

(1) Now I want you to break into groups of three...separate people. Well, you have to be careful; people start getting literal in there. I did this one time and someone's arm fell off. Of course, it wasn't a real arm, but I didn't know that. It scared me. They took a mannequin's arm and did it. When I said break into groups of three people, this wise guy pushed the arm and it fell out. It scared the shit out of me.

Those of you in literature land may literally divide your consciousness into appropriate parts for these exercises. You have that opportunity. That will bring another state of consciousness.

(2) One of you will do complex syntax for the left hemisphere. Use lots of negation, and all the words and phrases that have to do with time: before, after, during, while, as you stop yourself from preventing the fact that you're trying to continue, when. Use all the linkage words—all of that counts. The only difference is that you increase your tempo to about double that of the other person. That helps overload. Continue to place phrasing on their breathing so that it's even and smooth. Keep your intonation going down at the end of each sentence. Just double the speed at which you speak.

(3) The person will be talking to the right hemisphere about nursery rhymes. "Mary had a little lamb, its fleece was..." But only do part of them so that your subject has to finish them. Then give the person a little space by pausing; then add another

one. Tell the subject to see bits and pieces of visual memories from the past that they really, really enjoyed, lots and lots. Use childhood tonalities as much as you can. "Deeper go, trance in; sleep now; deeper sleep; sleep and sleep; eyes open, very alert, listening to Richard, now."

(4) As you do this, I want you to start with just the kinesthetic induction, match hands, apart, match, apart. Then say, "Close your eyes, let your hands go down at the same rate at which you drop *all the way* into a deep trance."

(5) At that point, I want you both to start talking. Once the person looks zoned all the way through the floor, one of you holds up his hand and one of you gives the instructions to go back, again, and find a place where the person had heightened awareness.

(6) Use experiences that will amplify hyperesthesia. For example, did you see the move "On Golden Pond?" How many of you have been outside and the colors were brighter? Time was moving slower? We all have experiences of heightened awareness. Tell the person to go and find the most heightened awareness he ever had.

(7) Once the person has it, amplify that awareness. Have him double it, then triple it, then quadruple it.

(8) When the person is internally experiencing things very slowly, tell him that, when you reach over and touch him, he's going to open his eyes and see the world more vividly. He'll be able to perceive more than ever before. Let your client do it for awhile. Then tell the person he'll be able to tap this ability whenever he wants to. Put the person back into trance and then wake him up. Do you understand? *Now*. Let's go do it.

Good Times Ahead

You can create new states of consciousness. You can take some task or situation. Decide on one of the ways to best take advantage of it. Design an ideal state of consciousness for it. Use submodalities.

Try some new feelings. You changed your beliefs in terms of what's possible to feel. You can amplify it, or dump it. You can feel it quickly or slowly. Now you can develop more influence.

Find something that's good. Take things like falling in love. Take things like appreciating your kids.

A famous comic once said, "You get a few good meals, good orgasms, good laughs, and other than that it's pretty much all work, so quit whining and get down to it." Some of us enjoy work. I enjoy it.

I remember when I built a house up in the mountains. I really got into building rock walls, and really enjoyed it. Everybody thought I was possessed. I liked fitting all those little rocks in.

It could have been anything. I could have been piling pennies on top of one another. Human beings do the oddest things.

Make it so the surface of your skin feels more. People talk about feeling kind of numb. We have a direct hypnotic technique. Instead of suppressing pain, the opposite. We take pleasure through the ceiling.

People seem to have so few types of good feelings. When people feel excited, they have one kind of excitement. For some people tingling starts in their stomach and spreads out. For some others it starts at the fingertips and their toes and works in. Play with passion, excitement, or just pure comfort and contentment. People could have fifteen, twenty, thirty different ways of doing each one.

Take a list of submodalities and start arbitrarily. If you feel things starting from the top, start from the bottom and work your way up. Amplify the good feelings you have. Better, create new orders of them. This increases the likelihood you'll have more good feelings. People repeatedly prove this out as one of the prime benefits of my workshops.

Make a language with two hundred euphonious words for every guttural one. You will hear more pleasant conversations. You will have more attractive, and more of the attractive ways to get information.

Sensational Exercise

Make new good feelings and then decide when to have them. Get a partner. Make up a whole new good feeling, one they haven't had, arbitrarily. Just x off submodalities. Then x off locations on your body. Start anywhere, work in any directions until you have a full, good body sensation. Let your whole body go into hyperesthesia. Then ask for decisions. "When do we want to feel this way?"

Lots of people, when they walk up to the door of their own house, get depressed. They might not know why. Maybe their spouse nags them. More nagging, and they get more depressed. If that instead made them turn around with a glimmer in their eye and made them start to feel excited in a whole new way, I bet their spouse wouldn't nag nearly as much and life would be better.

You got stuck, maybe on the freeway. Your blood pressure climbed toward the ceiling. Henceforth, sit back and say, "At last I have more time for myself." Settle down and daydream. Somebody will honk and remind you it's time to go. Works for me every time.

We have ways to make you all kinds of good feelings. People do not, kinesthetically, visually, or auditorally, have nearly as rich an internal world as is immensely possible. And the richer the internal world, the richer the external world.

I'm sure that Mozart didn't have scratchy little voices inside his head nagging, "You never practice the piano. This song sucks!" or fuzzy little pictures of the instruments of the orchestra, with tinny little sounds, queasy quivering stomach flutters and stuff.

The people who live life to the fullest fill themselves up from the inside. Hyperesthesia on the outside makes it so your skin can tremble and feel good. Hyperesthesia can fill your inside.

Learn how to slowly, so you don't go through threshold, slowly begin to amplify all the internal submodalities related to pleasure in any context. Apply them in contexts and combinations you've never used before. If human beings can learn to enjoy jumping out of airplanes, they could conceivably learn to enjoy themselves through anything.

I've worked with assembly lines. I've made it so all the employees went from hating their job to loving it. That speeds up their assembly line and decreases production defects. That makes them proud as well as happy.

Have they stayed stuck there for life? No. They feel happy and enjoy themselves. They think the universe is a friendly place. When they go home they feel motivated. They go to night school. They become forepersons because they smile. People like that.

Unions made time one of the reasons workers got promoted. Otherwise workers got promoted by whether or not they had any sparkle and enjoyed themselves. If they were fun to be around, people promoted them to hang around with them. If they were boring and dull, then they could only get promoted through seniority. With seniority, you get to the golden years and retire. But you got so used to feeling cranky you don't know how to do anything else. Then you die of a heart attack so somebody else can enjoy your money.

Everybody should make a choice about that. They should learn. People keep telling me, "Don't live your life the way you do. If you don't jog, you won't add ten years to your life. Eat this, stop that." I probably move around more in the course of a day than most people do. But I don't think cancer is caused by cigarettes, and I don't think it's caused by hamburger. I think it's caused by the inability of people to adapt to their environment.

When people look at the world and life as a challenge and keep their kinesthetics up and sensitive, they do adapt. I think they adapt at a genetic level.

When people whine and moan and flop around and make themselves feel bad while in even a friendly environment, then they do not adapt.

We can live anywhere. We have adapted. The vibrant energized human beings have adapted to whatever circumstances.

Good feelings are good for us. Make more of them.

IX

Reprogramming Limiting Decisions
A Walk Through Time

The phobia cure seemed unique in NLP. There's no elicitation involved. There also doesn't seem to be any meaningful relationship among the words you say when you use the technique. It's just that when you do these things with your mind there's no more phobia.

Time cruises on. Now we have an allergy cure. Someday maybe we can have a psychology cure.

For years psychologists told me that phobics have secondary gain. As a mathematician my initial response to that was, "Wow! Great!" But psychologists thought that was bad. Eventually I discovered that, for the most part, there is no secondary gain. There's just primary gain.

A lady had numb feet. So a psychiatrist friend called me and said, "Can you see a client today?" I said, "Why?" He said, "This lady just came in for treatment, this one is so great, you're going to love this one." Her feet would get numb and she would fall over.

A neurologist had checked her out and couldn't find any-thing. The numbness moved up and down, sometimes up to her ankles or even her knees. The neurologist explained, "There just aren't nerves in the right places for this to happen. It just doesn't fit neurology. It must be some kind of hysterical reaction."

So they brought this lady and her husband way up into the mountains where I lived at the time. The husband looked like kind of a redneck and spoke like an Oakie. He said, "Yeah, our marriage used to be real good, you know, but now with all the trouble she has standing up, I gotta do the dishes, and all the housework and cleaning. I have to go out and make all the money too. Do you think you can do something about it, doc?"

Every time he mentioned something like housework her smile got bigger and bigger. I call that primary gain.

I wanted to try some things with this lady. I figure that we can use symptoms as a form of communication. So I looked at her and used mixed-state communication. "I don't want to talk to you, I want to speak to your feet directly." I have no idea what that meant. But for some reason it seemed appropriate at the time—especially when she looked down at her feet and said, "Okay."

Then I said to her feet, "Now, I know you've been doing something useful for this lady. But you've been overzealous to prove to her how you're a benefit, because you've been numbing her feet all the time. What I want you to do instead, is make the numbing go away and only happen when you get the appropriate message...*now!*" She said, "They're not numb!" She had put up with this condition for ten years. Now she could walk. She could keep her balance.

I said, "Now, I want you to come back in a week and you'll know what the message is." Well, they went home and the psychiatrist called me. He said the husband told the lady, "It's your turn to do the dishes." She went numb up past her knees and started to fall. Talk about an unconscious with a sense of humor! And a sense of laziness.

Suggestive Decisions

All of us make decisions. We make some consciously. We make most decisions unconsciously. Even the decisions we make consciously go unconscious fast.

For instance, sometimes people decide they are unlovable. Sometimes they decide they won't be successful in life. Sometimes they decide they won't be good at things, or that they are not smart.

I know people who decided they are unmusical. You hear people say they "can't carry a tune." Wrong representation system! When people decide something like, "I am not musical," they begin to live in accordance with that decision. It becomes their internal map or model of the world.

Use time-lines in hypnotic work. You can regress people back to before they made those decisions. Then they can make a different decision. Bringing them up through time changes the meaning of their past experience. This satisfies the need for any secondary gain.

Unconscious Suggestions

When you bring people out of trance, be sure that you make permissive suggestions that allow the unconscious to fill all their needs magically, and that's the magic word.

A symptom is a representation of some needs being fulfilled and some not. The changes you make allow new needs to be met. You don't want it to happen at the expense of old needs. The unconscious can make adjustments that let things happen one way at one time and another way at another. That's the nature of the unconscious.

This is a great thing about Milton's way of doing hypnosis. He used permissive suggestions and thus allowed the client permission to respond. It's the same idea I used yesterday when I told the lady "to see something of importance for yourself." By using non-referential noun phrases, "like something, anything, now I want you to think of certain things from your past," you permit the best to emerge. These phrases *sound* specific. They allow you to remain artfully vague while allowing clients to find useful things that fit for them. Nobody knows a person better than his own unconscious.

It's hard to know exactly what's the best thing. But you can utilize the kinds of constructions detailed in the Appendix. These will allow you to learn to use language specifically while remaining artfully vague.

There's also a section in there on the use of presuppositions. Presuppositions are wondrous things.

If I brought someone up on stage and said, "Now, I don't know which of these two chairs you're going to sit in and go into a trance in, but the most important thing is that you enjoy the process." What is presupposed? That she is going to sit in the chair, and that she will go into a trance.

Using presuppositions, and allowing people to choose increases your effectiveness. You see, it doesn't matter to me which chair they go into a trance in. But this statement lets people begin to go into the mode of following commands and of making choices. When I work with people, I often have them *make choices* one right after another. Pick this. Pick something from the past. I don't tell them what.

Supposed

People can choose. Too many people do *supposed* to dos. In Britain I discovered a *disease* about it.

I wanted to buy a coat in one store. I said, "I will give you the money if you order me the coat." The guy said, "But I'm not supposed to do that." So I said, "You're a store and you're not supposed to take money?" He said, "Well, we ordered those coats before; I'm not supposed to order the same ones twice." I said, "But I want to buy the coat."

I also told people in the hotel when I wanted to have my room cleaned. I said, "Look, I want to have my room cleaned at five o'clock." The lady said, "But we're supposed to clean it first thing in the morning." I said, "Well, if you do, you have to carry me out of the room first. I want to have it cleaned at five. Aren't the maids here at five?" She said, "Yes." And I said, "Well, what do they do?" She said, "I don't know." And I said, "Well, tell them to come here." And she said, "But they're supposed to do it in the morning."

Now I thought rules are supposed to have a purpose. They wanted the rooms cleaned early so people would be *happy*, not so they could pester people! How many of you have stayed in a motel and had to fight the maid off?

Turning Timelines

Do you remember where your time-line is? For those of you who have the future in back and the past in front of you—you may find yourself somewhat in the past. Now you'll discover how time-lines provide immense value.

Doctors and drug counselors can discover this about junkies. You know of people who repeatedly get hooked on the same drug. Guess what? They have the past behind them and a short sighted future in front. They can't see themselves making the same mistake again. They get off the drug. They can still convince themselves to go back on it.

Have these people grab hold on to their time-line into the past and go *scrrreeechh* moving their past time-line into their vision. Have them hear the sound of a bolted door slamming shut. Have them see it whether they like it or not. Have them look at how many times they became a junkie and how productive it's made their lives. It's hard to build a really good life when smack got hooked on you.

So while agoraphobia may be a costly disease, being a junkie is more than expensive. You don't see many old heroin addicts.

You ever notice that? You see 90-year-old guys smoking and drinking, but you don't see them shooting heroin. It'll kill you; it's hard on you.

Timeline Redecision

Now I want you to close your eyes and see your own time-line. I want you to put the time-line in front of you. Then, literally, float up above it, in your mind, and float into the past. Now float back further and further and further. Keep moving down your time-line until you come to a time when you were very young.

Find some decision you made in the past that gets in the way in your life today, whether it's about money, sex, success, competence, whatever. Float way, way back until you can *literally* feel it getting stronger. The feelings that surround that decision will take you right back to the times and places where you made the decision that limits you.

Now, instead of dropping back into that event and reliving it, and therefore reinforcing it, stay above your time-line. I want you to float back a little bit further. Before you drop down, I want you to remember the strong beliefs you elicited and created for yourself. Staying above your time-line, I want you to pop up the beliefs that you're going to be the way you *would rather be*. When you pop it into your mind, I want you to drop down into your time-line, keeping that belief solid in your mind.

Then shoot all the way forward on your time-line, just like a rollercoaster. Days and weeks are passing before you, right through the old decisions, right up to the present. Pop out of the end of your time-line, float back and put it back where it was. Zoom right through that time-line. The faster you go, the more it will break up the old generalizations.

Now, as you come back, I want you to stop and think about your past decision and find out how it feels now. Try in vain to have it feel the same way. This is how you begin to blow up things from the past. Once you've done that, start to build futures. We're going to spend time on that this afternoon: "juicing up your future."

Amplifying Your Resources in Your Future

This section involves taking the pieces you have learned and putting them together. In NLP we talked about "future pacing." Today we do *mega* compared to how we used to teach it. We used to have people think of something for which they need more resources, anchor positive responses, have them think of that experience or event in the future, and fire the resource anchor.

We're going to do that today, but multiplied a hundred times. We're going to take your hypnotic skills and five of the most powerful responses you've ever had. I want you to think about the new decision you made. Think about the contexts where that decision will apply in your future.

Redecision on a Timeline Demonstration

You sir. First, tell me where your time-line is. Where's the future? Off in that direction; to your right. And where's your past? Does it go kind of diagonally in front of you?

You will want to know this about your client. Knowing this will allow you to orient him better. Now we are ready to induce an altered state.

Do you know what kind of decision you want to change and the new decision you want to install in its place? Good. Now think of what will let you know when the right contexts are occurring in your mind. Let yourself become aware of the things that are going to happen in the future that create the context.

Now I want you to think of five personal resources that you would really like to have. Of course, you have some of them already to a certain degree. Some people already have confidence. What if you had that and others, and they were *intensely stronger* and all there at the same time? You would be able to do what you need to do *dynamically*.

I want you to put those five resources in your mind now. If this person's time-line has the future here and the past there, I'm going to take these five responses—one, two, three, four, five—and put them in the future. Then I'm going to have you repeat them. But I'm going to put them closer and closer together, so eventually they all occur at the same time.

Then we are going to program this person so that *the more he goes* into the future, *the more* these five powerful responses will occur simultaneously. This builds up a recursive loop that will strengthen their responses.

But the first thing I have to do is get him into a trance. Then I want to *access* each of the five responses and really amplify them. Trance has a tendency to both focus attention and amplify responses anyway.

Have any of you ever seen stage hypnotists? For one routine they say, "I'm going to show you a shoe and it's going to make you really sad." Then when they show the person a shoe, he bursts into tears. Hypnosis can have the same effect as hormones that get "out of control." Everything gets intensified.

The stage hypnosis tricks don't seem very valuable. Use hypnosis to find personal resources and amplify them. That's valuable.

Today we are going to sensorama-land! Have you been in sensorama theaters with the 160-foot screens and Dolby stereo? They put the speakers on the floor so when they show the movie *Earthquake* the building actually shakes. Do they have those over here? We'll build one in your head. It'll save you at least two dollars and seventy-five cents each showing.

Amplifying Resources Demonstration

I want you to sit here and let your unconscious do the work. That's right. Because I'm going to take your hand like this. I'm going to lift it up just like this, straight out in front of you, and I'm not going to tell you to put it down. *Right now* I want you to slowly begin to slide deeper and deeper into trance.

I want your hand, involuntarily, to float up toward your face, *feeling* an attraction between your thumb and your nose—an attraction to new learning. As you begin to go much deeper, now, taking a deep breath, straighten out your head. I want you to let your head float up straight as if you can feel gravity in the center of it. Feel it floating down evenly, all the way around so you stay balanced. Because you're going to learn things that will balance out your future.

As you sit there, I want you…very slowly, as your hand goes toward your face, to begin to go back to that childlike state of wonder; that state where you really could learn things that imprinted in your mind and stayed with you for the rest of your life; that state when you were fascinated by the smallest things, and everything was so dramatic that it stayed with you forever.

I want you to go into your life and find the first of your five resources. Go into the time that your conscious mind might have forgotten. Go to the most *dramatic* example of when you had that resource, and see it right now. That's right. I want it to get bigger and bigger; feel it more and more dramatically until it fills your whole body. That's right. Stronger, more intensely; turn up the volume, turn up the brightness, and feel it each time you feel this now.

As your hand continues toward your face I want you to move into that second response. Let your unconscious find something that you perhaps haven't thought about in years. Let your unconscious be your guide and show it to you *now.* That's right. See it. Make it bigger and brighter and stronger. Keep doing it until it fills your whole body. Turn it *way* up right now. Double it. That's right. And double it again. That's the stuff that men are made of. *Yahhhahh!* There you go.

As you go deeper into a trance, it's time for number three. Let your unconscious pick a dramatic example, and see it now. That's right. Turn it up and double it and double it, louder, brighter, bigger, *sensorama-land!* Now double it again. *Brrahhhhhahh!* There you go. When you feel that power, that's the power you're going to combine with other things later on.

Now it's time to go to number four. We're going to do this a little bit differently, though. In a moment, I'll ask you to let your hand turn slowly and form a cup like this, and to let it move up. In a moment I want you to open your eyes. You will see something in your hand that you haven't thought about in years.

See a time when you had that response. You will see yourself in your hand with that resource. And when you begin to see it more clearly than you ever imagined, it's going to jump right out of your hand. When I touch the back of your hand, that resource will jump into your self and into your future. Let your eyes open and see it now. That's right. There you go...and close your eyes. Let that resource fill your body; double it and double it. Let it move up to your arms and legs and grow stronger inside you. You can feel that anytime you want it.

Now it's time to move on to number five. For number five I want your unconscious to pick a doozy! I want it to show it to you...that's right, *now. Yahhhaahh!* You see it and feel it every time you think, "Your ass is mine!" That's right. Who says trance has to be boring? I've heard that from people. They say, "But he laughed, he couldn't have been in a trance." But you can laugh yourself deeper and deeper into a trance. *Ahhhhha.* All the way down. That's right.

What I want you to do now is float up in your mind, above your time-line. Float up and look off into the future. Position yourself so that you're looking down on events that haven't occurred yet. That's right.

Now take each of the five responses and put them a week apart into the future. Then I want you to put the same five four days apart. Then three days apart, two days, one day, and then one hour apart until they blend together in the future.

Then I want you to float down very slowly inside your time-line and *bullet forward* into the future and shoot out the end. And do it *nnnnoooowwwww!* That's right.

Feel all those resources come together inside you in a powerful way. When that's finished, I want you to float back and put your time-line right back where it was. Let all those resources blend together; feel them combine and spread until you feel a tingling at your midline as the resources begin to fit together, so that every time you see a context in which you need those resources you will feel their power and you will remember the giggle that goes with it. That's right. And you'll say, "Your ass is mine!" There you go.

When your unconscious knows that you have integrated these things, and takes responsibility for making them a part of your future experience, your hand will float down. When it touches your knees, your eyes will open and your internal voice will say with total authority, "Piece of cake!" That's right. Take all the time you need.

Test Your Work

Do you get the general idea? It's to take the resources that exist inside of people, and not only use them, but amplify them. Use tonality for this. It's important. Be congruent in what you say. When you say, "bigger, brighter and stronger" let the congruency in your voice move people to get the feelings to spread maximally throughout their bodies. Then, when they get this response, they viscerally feel the power inside them.

Many people don't do half of what they want to do or could do in their lives. Often they just haven't felt the power of what they need in order to do these things.

I find that especially true when I teach my flirting class. The toughest part of flirting is getting people to walk across the room. I did this with a football team. I know you think that football players have guts. I'll tell you, when it comes to talking to girls, these guys didn't yet. They could go out and bang heads until they were blue in the face. But when I said, "Go over and say hello to this woman," they would look at me with terror in their eyes. "What?" They can do anything. They shoot guns and fight wars. But to go over and say hello? No!

For them to *overcome* that kind of fear seems very hard. Besides, overcoming rarely motivates people. The way to empower people to do things is to build the resources so that people feel *impelled and compelled* to do them. When people look at somebody across the room I want them to want to say hello and to feel unable to sit still. I want to build a compulsion to use these new learnings, *now,* so that the compulsion fires off automatically. Then, when the context arises, the feelings will grow so strong that people will be able to do it without hesitation.

How do you feel sir?

"Great."

Now, here's a test. Get in the habit of testing your work. Remember that I asked you before you started to think of a future context where you would need this.

Now I want you to stop and think of the context you thought of before, and find out what happens. So what happens? How do you feel about it?

"Great."

Great? That's pretty good. You have mastered understatement. You lived your whole life in London. What do English women do when they have orgasms? Do they look at guys and say, "Well, that was a bit of okay." Haven't you ever watched Tony the Tiger?

"It's *grrreeaattt!*"

Thank you.

Now, I know it's not terribly British, but you need to use your tone of voice to *re-elicit* the power responses, and when you crank them up, when you've hit the ceiling, then *double it again*.

You can do it anywhere, anytime. You can start before you were born. You can continue as long as you can imagine. Now.

Epilogue

We are already in a trance. You might happen to be in one that you're used to. If you like you can think of your every belief as a post hypnotic suggestion with its own mini-trance. You can think of any trance as a set of beliefs that happen to be operating at the moment.

Any particular trance will offer results we like in some situations. Any belief will pay off in some circumstances. Keep them that way. Otherwise they tend to contradict each other.

Acting in accord with suggestions and beliefs may be useful or not. It depends. Acting in accord with contradictions tends to short circuit your brain and your life.

Whenever you do hypnosis, do two things. Do one inside, with yourself, and one outside, with them. Actually, do the same thing both ways.

You can start out incongruent, and pace incongruence. Lead yourself into unanimity. They have mixed feelings. They have confused pictures. Their internal dialogue speaks incongruently. I, congruent, tell them with every fiber of my soul, "That's not going to be the way it is." Tune yourself, every cell of yourself, to transmit in concert. Learn to take any dissonance into harmony, melody. Get jazzed.

Work with people, with them. Especially if you do anything supposedly educational, like therapy or sales. Use what they've got. People have told me for years and years, "Compulsives are the hardest people to work with." Nonsense.

Compulsives will do anything you tell them. Threaten them, "If you don't follow these instructions your life will be ruined." Then make them 10 or 20 pages of detailed instructions of things to do for the first hour of every day, and then keep going. Have them come back in two weeks. Check how they did. They expect you to back off. Say, "Now I want you to double the amount of time you do all these things. Or now, then life will be…" Then you threaten them again.

That's how they function. They become your most dedicated clients. They don't just get better. They go from basket cases to the most organized, efficient fun-lovers. Those instructions include, "You will spend five minutes planning how to enjoy yourself, and how you can improve your tonality, and how you can smile better, and what you can do for your health, and organize, and plan." After doing all this detail, then they carry it out.

Taking things as problems and viewing people as broken has remained the whole premise of psychologists. They look for wrong. So they tell people, "I read this book by this Grandler Brindler guy, and this is supposed to work with people. So we'll give it a try and see if you're one of those whose phobia can go away." Immediately they think, "I'm not one of the ones." You can look them straight in the eye and say, "I'll bet you think you're not one of those ones." They start to smile. The minute you can get them to laugh marks the minute you can get them to change. It's predictable.

Human behavior is not erratic. Human behavior is systematic. It has to be. It does not have to be repetitive and destructive.

It amazed me that people did the same thing, again, when it's unpleasant. You know, for somebody to want to enjoy life, to go out and become a serial killer, to have to live on the run, to have to plot and plan. If they went through all that they could find something productive and pleasant to do. But it's a statement about what we quibble about in this culture, and it's a statement about our educational system.

We quibble about whether or not we should have the right to run other people's rights. We pass laws about what you can put into your body, what you can do with your body. Rich old white men lay down the law what poor young black girls can do with their own bodies. We passed the amendment to the constitution to keep religions out of the law, yet they snuck in.

Today, in California, you're not allowed to go to a bar after 2 o'clock. Why? In Salt Lake City you could barely drink, but you could have all the wives you wanted. This is not what our founding fathers had in mind.

We all believe different things. Anything idiosyncratic shouldn't cross the line. I shouldn't be able to influence your life, you shouldn't be able to influence mine, except by mutual consent, or by setting a good example and demonstrating.

When human beings get together they want rules about what to do and how to do it with each other. The rules become laws. The advent of law brings lawyers. The lawyers become politicians.

In the beginning, the U.S. constitution established free rights for all MEN. Not women, not blacks, not Chinese, but the Irish, well, yes. How can we sort this crap out? I don't know. But, then, it was all clear to them.

As time goes by we'll track the one thing they had that made everything work. Personal rules of a group contradict those of other groups. Rules that work well enough persuade people. That influences and leads people. Then you don't have to force it on them. So don't.

Some say, "If people could have abortions then they'll be running around doing it everywhere." On the contrary, the minute people start doing something they start caring. Laws against an immoral act lead to laws against knowing or spreading information about it. By contrast, if somebody robs banks or drives on the wrong side of roads, the law says to let everyone know. We have laws against women finding out how to get what they want done with their own bodies. With laws that legislate personal morality, people act from opposition or agreement, instead of from caring and knowing.

Everybody's got a point of view. We all see and don't see different things. Nobody's always going to get everything right. Start out with that premise.

Clients say they want to get rid of things. One wanted to get rid of all his anger. I thought, "What if people walk on his face?" Then he'll go to assertiveness training. He has to go to assertiveness training to get anger again. Then he'll beat up his wife. He has to go through bioenergetics to release the anger. He thought, "Get rid of anger. That will solve everything." How did that start? Learn to use anger. Learn the value of things.

It boils down to this: People have got to learn to make better decisions. Keep that inside of everything here. Change beliefs to improve the quality of decisions.

Junkies can go through years, decades, of total horribleness. They get dried out. They walk out of the Betty Ford Clinic or a halfway house. They run into somebody who asks, "Want to shoot up?" They say, "Wow, what a great idea!" Whap! They do addiction again. How can they? It shows me that they don't make good decisions. They don't think, "I don't have enough holes in my body already. Take this device and make new ones." They only think of the rush. They don't let enough time inside of deciding. They think, "Oh, I'll get this big rush." They could let their mind run through years like they already had. They'd turn around and look and say, "No, I don't think so."

What got them into the problem in the first place? They based decisions on short term pictures, talk, and feelings. Some people run way ahead. It comes out better. But not when they make the decision on something short.

I know a guy that used to never go out on dates. He walked up to me and said, "I'm thinking of going out on a date next fall." He told me in January. I looked at him and asked, "Anybody in particular?" He said, "Well, I'm considering it." And I asked, "What happens when you think about walking up to any old girl and saying, 'Would you like to go out?' If she says yes, you say, 'I'll see if I can find somebody for you.'" He just looked at me, crazy Richard.

Whenever he thought about going out with somebody, he ran all the way through, until they were 80 years old, including, when they were 35, and had kids, she died, and it was horrible. He'd think, "It's too much trouble." He didn't even get to talk to them. He did too much. He just wanted to go have a few drinks. He confused too many subjects together.

People in trance respond in the moment and literally, and they respond appropriately. If you take a person who's not a junkie, and say, "Here's a hypodermic needle and a lot of heroin. Would you like to become an addict?" They'll say, "No." Hypnotists, for decades, have tried to come up with ways to get you to violate your beliefs. Actually, people in trance make better decisions. They slow down and take the time to do it, instead of kicking off the automatic ones. They don't fall into the old pattern of behavior. They cruise at a different speed. They notice things they ordinarily would not.

Sometimes you don't have so much ecstasy in a situation. Try going through it at different speeds in your mind. Floor the accelerator. Touch the brakes. It's your brain. There's no one behind you and nothing to run into. Put it in reverse. Run your universe backwards. Find a good direction. Try a little arbitrary flexibility.

In the beginning I talked about riding on a beam of light. Your experience depends upon where you look at it from. Add the dimension of, not only your location and velocity in the external world, but the internal world as well. Ride that beam of light. How fast does your mind go while you're doing it?

Speed your mind up to twice the speed of light. You'll feel like you move slowly. Anybody who's ever driven a car on the freeway in LA and gotten off going 40 miles an hour knows that. Anybody who's waited in line at the bank knows that. You know, you can stand there and the person in front of you takes forever. You look at your watch and only a minute has gone by. It seems like half an hour has transpired.

We need to learn to switch this stuff around. When you go in line at the bank it goes by like that. When it's time to have an orgasm, it takes half an hour, not have one, but for the moment to have transpired.

We can put our worlds in good order. We need only learn. The world will make this worth our while. We need only teach people how to have a good time and do some good in the world. We had better learn well. We teach dreck. We have laws to tell us how to behave and schools to tell us what to believe. That makes two disasters.

Give everybody the widest range that we have. Start people off with the ability to learn and believe, like Einstein. We're starting our children off having those beliefs, and whipping them out by teaching stupid things like phonic spelling. Phonetics is a good way to learn to read. It's a very poor way to learn to spell. And it doesn't teach you about writing, and it doesn't account for things.

The school district told my kids that they couldn't use calculators. They said, "It wouldn't really teach them to learn." I said,

"Hogwash." Then they said it wouldn't be fair to the others. So I got every kid a calculator. Finally the teacher asked, "Can you teach me how to use it?"

The answers are in the teacher's book. As long as the answers are in the teacher's book and not the kid's book, we'd better get down to teaching the teachers. Our educational system is a disaster, and no amount of money can fix it. It is not a problem with money.

I teach hundreds of people all the time, and I have no problem. I've had groups of 100 children, and I never had any problem. "But," they ask, "How long could you keep that up?" I've been keeping it up for twenty years with kids and adults and everybody else. It's not how many people there are, it's the environment that you create for them.

The environment should relate to what's going on. The fact that they don't have computers in every classroom is ludicrous. Even if they have to tell the parents, buy them one. They're not that expensive anymore. Good God, people throw them away. They're like tin cans now. There's ample opportunity for all these things to be available. We should start creating rich environments. We've got to start with the teachers.

We have people teaching who not only don't know, they don't suspect and they can't learn. They are there for the wrong reasons. The few good teachers that exist in almost every school spend all their time getting persecuted. And we all know this is true, but nobody addresses the problem.

It's always about money. No. The kids can write their own books and bring their own computers. It's not a function of money, it's not a function of the building. It's a function of the fact that we have not hired qualified people, and we don't have them doing the right job.

Tenure was an important part of protecting teachers. It backfired. Good teachers don't get tenure. Most tenure goes to the people that really should get a people-free job. Or else we should get them to like what they're doing.

Through the years I've seen, in my teaching, all the professions on the face of the earth, to plumbers and electricians. The least that I get from any single profession who come and learn from me is teachers. And it ain't because I criticize them.

I get psychologists up the yin-yang, and I really give them a bad time. But they want to learn. They just went to places where nobody taught them. They learned your legs crossed means you're closed to ideas. That's stupid. Ideas don't go up that hole. Although many people seem as if most did most of the time.

You need to be able to open up the doorways. One of the best ways to do that is to get people to stop talking, start listening. And that's all hypnosis is. Focus your attention, go into another state, try a new way, try it another new way. We have begun to learn what we can do.

We can teach our children faster and better than ever before and make it more fun. We have the research to prove it. And the next generation had better be the best creators and problem solvers ever on the face of the earth or we're in deep, and I don't mean hypnosis.

You may feel afraid. People often felt scared of using hypnosis because it meant losing control. You know hypnosis can give you control. Various states of trance can give you control of things you didn't know existed. Maybe that was the real fear all along. If not, you might choose to add that fear. You can control the flow of your blood and of your time. Make wise choices. You are discovering new worlds.

Why did the little rock and roll musician who did computer programming find out all this? I didn't know any better. I thought, "When you get your car fixed, it runs better afterwards. If it doesn't, bring it back and punch somebody."

I wanted to make better training programs. I asked people questions. I wanted to model their expertise. We had all these books, watched all these people. Nobody could tell me anything of which you could say, "I'm cursed," and they'd say, "Bibbity Bobbity Boo," and you'd leave without it. Not one.

Psychiatrists at the time had the highest suicide rate. No wonder. Their field did not have one thing. Not only that, they sat around and let their clients hypnotize them.

This book includes quick techniques for good results. You have no excuse to practice these techniques if you don't have the tonality to go with it, if you don't have the tempo, and if you don't use it on yourself first. Rule one is go first. If you ain't happy, cheer up. Any way you ain't working, get yourself fixed before you touch anybody else.

Sex therapists come to me either impotent or frigid. Why do they do sex therapy? That makes no sense.

Most teachers aren't good learners. They should make themselves good learners. Learn more kinds of learning than book learning.

What we can learn from this book serves only to guide. We can use the techniques in here. We need to know that every time we do we can do it better. There's always a quicker, faster, gentler way. Just where you stand is important.

In the future books like *Design Human Engineering* will explain not only the tonalities to use, but where to stand and how to move. We've got down now to begin to use these kinds of things. We use holophonic mikes and create environments for people to learn skills. We've learned that the more nearly the simulator resembles the experience, the more people will learn. It applies to tasks like maneuvering in orbit, repairing nerves in surgery, and driving cars.

We haven't built a simulator yet for what all of this is about, the plethora of unexplored states of consciousness for every human being. Create more. You have time.

—Richard Bandler with Janus Daniels

Appendix 1

Accessing Cues

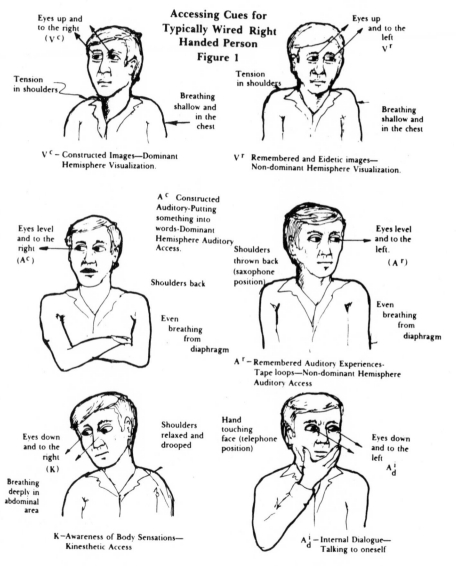

Accessing Cues for Typically Wired Right Handed Person
Figure 1

Eyes up and to the right (V ^{c})

Tension in shoulders

Breathing shallow and in the chest

V ^{c} – Constructed Images—Dominant Hemisphere Visualization.

Eyes up and to the left V ^{r}

Tension in shoulders

Breathing shallow and in the chest

V ^{r} Remembered and Eidetic images—Non-dominant Hemisphere Visualization.

A ^{c} Constructed Auditory-Putting something into words-Dominant Hemisphere Auditory Access.

Eyes level and to the right (A ^{c})

Shoulders back

Even breathing from diaphragm

Shoulders thrown back (saxophone position)

Eyes level and to the left (A ^{r})

Even breathing from diaphragm

A ^{r} – Remembered Auditory Experiences-Tape loops—Non-dominant Hemisphere Auditory Access

Eyes down and to the right (K)

Breathing deeply in abdominal area

Shoulders relaxed and drooped

K—Awareness of Body Sensations—Kinesthetic Access

Hand touching face (telephone position)

Eyes down and to the left A $_d^i$

A $_d^i$ – Internal Dialogue—Talking to oneself

Accessing cues for typically wired right-handed person. Any behavioral cue that indicates processing of a certain sensory system is called an accessing cue.

Appendix 2

The Meta Model

I. Introduction

Learning the Meta Model is essentially learning how to hear and identify patterns in people's language.

I'll present the patterns and talk a little about them and then we'll break up into groups and practice them.

The Meta Model is probably one of the most important things to learn as a professional communicator because it is a way to gather high-quality information from the people that you are working with, no matter what kind of field you are in.

I will start with a story about gathering information and the Meta Model:

I was up in Canada doing a workshop on hypnosis with a group of people and there was a gentleman there who was a hypnotist. He told us a story that was very interesting. He said that at one time he had this woman come in as a client. He sat her down and he did some hypnotic tests. She seemed to be a good subject and he had good rapport with her. He started off doing this induction, with his most refined Ericsonian techniques, using tonal markings, embedded commands, and all those various things. After about half an hour she was still sitting there with her eyes open and nothing was happening. He finally stopped and said, "Gee, I don't understand what is going on. You seem to have good susceptibility, and there seems to be good rapport. I can't find any reason for it, but you don't seem to go into a trance very easily. Is everything all right?" So, she says to him, "Well, you haven't shown me one of those things yet." He asks, "What things?" and she says, "You know, the crystal ball." He says to himself, "That's one of those pieces of archaic paraphernalia that old-time hypnotists used," but he thinks he has one back in his drawer that he used to use for stage demonstrations. So he goes rummaging through his bottom drawer.

He reaches way in the back of the drawer and pulls out this pendulum sort of thing, and he says, "You mean this?" and holds it up. She goes, "Yes," and collapses immediately into a deep trance... (Laughter).

I had an experience that was very much like that when I was working with a woman on weight control. I elicited her strategy and tried to program in a new strategy using anchoring and stuff like that. I thought I did a nice job, but she came back a week later and says, "Well, it worked a little bit, but I am still not having much success." I couldn't figure it out. Finally, I asked her if she had ever changed a problematic behavior before. And she said, "Well, I was sort of expecting that you would do this thing that this dentist did to me once." I said, "And what, specifically, was that?" And she goes on to tell me the story about how she used to be so nervous going to the dentist's office until one day the dentist got frustrated trying to work on her and said, "I'll have to do hypnosis with you!" She said he just grabbed on to her wrist and told her over and over how she would be comfortable the next time she came in. And she said, "I didn't go into a deep trance or anything like that, but I was sure surprised the next time I came in. I wasn't nervous at all." So, after I talked to her for a while, I just reached down and said the exact same thing he did. I used the same kind of intonation she used when imitating her dentist. I held her wrist and said, over and over, "You will have no trouble with your eating patterns this week and will lose weight comfortably." Then I told her that she'd just been in a hypnotic trance that would cure her weight problem, and to go home and call me in a week. She called back a week later and said, "Wow, this is great. This is just what I wanted. I've lost eight pounds already." The point is that I tried doing various techniques with little success until I asked for the information I needed. Then, she literally told me what I needed to do in order to make a change, because she had a reference experience.

Now, for me, this is what the Meta Model is all about: being able to increase your efficiency in anything by finding out that kind of specific information. Knowing anchoring, knowing strategies, or any technique by itself isn't going to get you anywhere unless you know *how* and *when* to use them. I could have done my best piece of strategy work with this woman, but there was something else that she wanted, one thing that she needed before she was willing to respond, just like the lady who was working with the hypnotist. For me, the Meta Model is all about asking these kinds of questions. What do you need? What would happen if you did? And that kind of stuff.

II. Development of the Meta Model

For those of you who haven't had experience with it before, I would like to start off from the beginning and take you down through the Meta Model ages.

It was first developed by John Grinder and Richard Bandler. In fact, this was the very first thing that they developed together. All the rest of NLP was discovered and developed by asking these questions. So this should be a good motivation for you. While there are other techniques, everything was precipitated by the Meta Model—which is simply asking questions. It is simply gathering information and questioning.

John and Richard started by studying Virginia Satir and Fritz Perls. In trying to find out what these therapeutic wizards did, they noticed that these therapists asked certain kinds of questions. Now, John was a linguist. He had all these neat categories in his head. He had studied this kind of stuff in college. But they were basically just academic things for him. Then he got together with Richard, and they put together this model that applied linguistic knowledge to actual behavior.

It is all based on the idea that *the map is not the territory*.

In order to operate on the world we all make maps of what is going on out there with our sensory apparatus, our eyes, ears, noses, mouths, and bodies. We also make maps of those maps, or models of those models, with our language systems. We call this a Meta Model, a model about modeling.

Now, we do this mapping with language. In other words, we map out our experience through language. Words are anchors for experience. A word is as much an anchor as a squeeze on the knee. Words tend to be the most common anchoring system, because there are so many changes that you can make in tonal qualities and the various phonological things that you can do with your mouth and lips. It is a very refined anchoring system. As far as I can tell, you organize words to trigger experiences and you use words in the same way that you would use tactile anchors. These words serve as a map for our internal maps, which are maps of the territory around you. So you are three places removed from the territory, the reality.

Now, John and Richard were always more interested in form, in the patterns of language, than in the content. They noticed that as people map their experience they have to leave certain things out. In other words, you are never going to get a truly explicit map.

There is a story about the cartography department of a small European village. The cartography department, the mapping department, was their biggest civic pride and they spent a lot of time on their maps. They decided that they would make a map that was perfect. They started making this map, and as they did it, they had to gather extensive amounts of information. The next thing they knew, they had to make the building bigger to store it all. But they kept refining their map, making it more and more detailed and pretty soon they just had to break down the walls of this building, laying out their maps all over the place. Of course, what finally happened was that the map got so big, it covered the territory completely.

The thing is, you don't need a map that big. As a matter of fact, it is okay to delete things. If you just want to find some street, it is okay to just use a street map that deletes information like hills, and deletes what kind of trees and what kind of foliage is around. However, if you are concerned about areas to plant, and what kind of soil is around, you will want to look for a different kind of map.

People that use only visual predicates are doing this kind of thing that we are talking about with their representational systems. They are using a predicate that describes one portion of the territory–the visual aspect of that territory. Other people describe just the kinesthetic aspects, other people the auditory, and so on.

The major pattern that I am leading up to is what we call *deletion*.

A. Deletion

Deletion: that is just leaving something out. As I said, you can't make a map without leaving something out unless you want to make yourself ridiculous. You can't possibly describe in detail all of your experiences. So you start leaving things out. The only problem with that is that sometimes you delete information that is important. You have to find the right information for the right map. Most of you have heard language patterns such as, "I'm scared ...," "I'm confused...," or "I'm bewildered," or "I'm happy." And each of those patterns deletes certain portions of what you are describing. In some cases it is to your advantage to be able to recover some of that information. Those words, "happy," "confused," "bewildered," and "scared," are in a class of words called predicates. They are action words–they describe relationships between things. A word like "scared" is a two place predicate. What I mean by "place" is that it is describing an action between two things. So, someone is scared of something, and that has been deleted in the utterance, "I'm scared." So, of course, if you want to recover that information, your response would be, "Scared of what, specifically?" or, "What is it that scares you?" Similarly, if a person says, "I'm confused," he has to be confused about something.

In a sentence such as, "John ordered coffee and Mary ordered peas," it is okay to delete some information. Sometimes it is redundant. You don't need to say "ordered" twice, although you do have to be careful of the ambiguity in that particular phrase. If John ordered coffee and Mary peas…(laughter). What I am trying to say is that it is okay to delete some information, but other times deleted information is critically important. A professional communicator needs to be able to hear deletions when they occur and have the verbal tools to recover the deleted information when necessary.

One of the things we are going to be doing is trying to identify where people delete information that is important. For instance, if someone says that they're scared, it is very important to me to know what they are scared of. Or, if someone says that they are in pain, to know what is causing them that pain, and how it is causing them pain. Most of you will probably have intuitions about this. When someone deletes something, you say, "What specifically?" You will want to find out that kind of information.

1. Comparatives and Superlatives

There is another class of deletion that I want to talk about. If I were to say, "the Meta Model is the *best* way to gather information," I would be using the superlative, "best." You might want to ask, "Better than what? Compared to what?" If I say things like, "This is really good, this is great, this is far out, this is bad, terrible, or wrong," you will want to say, "Compared to what?" or, in response to the words for "better" and "worse," "Better than what. Worse than what?" This way, you get some kind of idea of how the person is making his comparisons. and how much information he has gathered before making that comparison. Many comparisons are a form of deletion.

B. Unspecified Referential Index

An unspecified referential index is any non-referring noun phrase; when you delete "whom" or "what." "They," who specifically? "This way," which way specifically? That statement is not specific enough. "It," and "people," are words used when you are deleting the specific person or object. Unspecified referential indices can be collective nouns, like, "people," "Neuro-Linguistic Programming," or "geniuses."

Politicians use this kind of language all the time. If you do you can get by with saying the same things Thomas Hobbes said. He said, "*Man* is basically antagonistic." You can get away with generalizing and distorting things by using a collective noun such as "man," but if you say, "every person," and you begin to name everybody, and challenge the generalization, it isn't going to fit, because you are going to realize that this is a big generalization. I find that using these kinds of collective nouns can get pretty slippery if you are not aware of the deletion. When I first learned the *meta model* (I was studying politics at the time), the very first thing I did with it was to apply it to Plato's dialogues because of all the different ways that Socrates manipulates and uses language, deletes and distorts, and presupposes. Socrates just spins people around, because he was really good with violating and utilizing meta model patterns.

C. Nominalizations

Nominalization: Most of you have probably had some sort of experience with this word. A nominalization means that you take something that is an action, a *process,* and you *turn it into a noun*–that is a static entity or object. A typical one is something like "freedom..." To say "I lost my freedom" is like saying, "I lost my wallet." You are treating freedom as if it were a thing. Similarly, saying, "The tension built in the room" is like saying, "The carpenter built in the room." You can confuse the word, tension, with something that is a thing and not the process of somebody being tense about something.

So, in a way, nominalization is a form of deletion, too, because you are deleting certain information about the process you are talking about; specifically in this case, tension or freedom. Being free to do what, specifically? Someone may say, "I am having trouble with my *life,*" or, "Things are going wrong in my *life.*" Well, you can break that down. You want to turn it around and make it into a process. Living where? With whom? And, living how? You know, life is not a thing. And so, what you do with a nominalization is try and take this action or activity used as a noun or a thing and bring it back into a process. If someone says, "I am having a lot of difficulty with this relationship," you ask, "Relating to whom?" You put it back into the verb form of "relate."

One of the ways to identify these kinds of things for yourself is to pay attention to your own internal representation of what the person says. So, if I say, "Yesterday I had an accident...," does everybody understand what I am saying? Careful, I could have crashed down the stairs, I could have tripped into somebody, I could have forgotten something. I would like to get a couple of people's responses to that question. When I said, "an accident," who thought of what? What did you think of? Answer: "I cut my finger." (Robert) "Was it verbal like that?" (Answer) "No, I saw a cut finger." (Someone else) "I pictured an automobile accident." (Someone else) "Bowel movement…(laughter)."

Essentially, what I am saying is that, here, I used a phrase that everybody made sense of. You could understand that verbalization, but you each had different representations. As I've always said, "A word is worth a thousand pictures."

One of the things that always has amazed me is that people in therapeutic contexts, and people in business contexts, very often don't realize that. In other words, you listen to somebody say they had an accident, or "I am really troubled," and you make sense of that for yourself without really knowing the other person's representation for it.

Some people are very prone to nominalizations. Many people have what we call *blind spots* to meta model patterns. I was once in a workshop and there was a woman there who used nominalizations like crazy. She would say, "I just don't understand why my experiences and realizations don't contribute to the actualization of my frustrations in a direction that will cause an integration of my life crisis." To make a teaching point I replied, "Because of the experiential qualities of your learnings and understandings, you begin to formulate new perceptions of childhood conceptualizations and knowledge…" and spewed out about five minutes worth of crap, and she goes, "Oh, yeah, that is what I was thinking too." She made sense out of what I said. Everyone just started laughing because I had just sat there for five minutes thinking of all the nominalizations that I could, and she made sense of it.

If somebody just keeps going on and following what another person is saying, and, internally, makes up his own map for what that other person is saying, that map has nothing to do with what the other person is talking about. There is a phenomenon called transderivational search.

1. Transderivational Search

Transderivational search means you search back through your experiences to find a reference for what I am talking about. If you had done a transderivational search when I said, "I had an accident," you would have gone back through your personal history until you had found a reference structure for accidents. You might have gone back to an automobile accident in which you participated. That word "accident" is an anchor to trigger for a bunch of representations in your personal history, your experience. In one seminar, I asked for people's representations for the word "dog" and somebody burst into tears, because the day before her dog had died. It got hit by a car. Those kinds of things can easily happen, because words are anchors. People will refer to their own experiences to make sense of someone else's.

Now, as any one of you who has worked with hypnotic patterns know, you use the exact opposite of the meta model when you are doing a trance induction. For instance, you take the process of nominalization and use it rampantly, because you know people will follow along anyway. So, I go along and am talking about "incorporating these new learnings and understandings in a way that is the most meaningful to you in your life today." Now, that doesn't mean anything. What are learnings? Somebody learning something specifically, through understanding what? And you want to use these to influence and create 4-tuples in that person. I've been doing this to all of you during this presentation.

Now, again going back to the meta model treatment of language, what you want to do with a nominalization is to make sure that it goes back into the process and then you recover what has been deleted. So, *what you do with a nominalization is put it back into process.*

Q: What if a client says there are bad *vibes* at his office?

A: "Vibes" is a nominalization. How would you put that back into process? What you want to ask is, "What vibrating about what?" What is vibrating, and what is causing it to vibrate?" So you take the nominalization and bring it back into a verb. "Vibrating how, specifically?"

Let's say I say something like, "My love for you is growing." How could you put that back into process? "Loving, how?" Try a sentence that didn't delete who you were loving.

You say, "I can't deal with my confusion." I respond, "What are you confused about? And how is it confusing you?" You want to put "confusion" back into a verb form, which is to make it a process again. Question: "How about making it reflexive? For instance, how are you confusing yourself?" Answer: That is presupposing that they *are* making themselves confused. That would be a pretty big presupposition, but you can get a lot of information and sort of get them thinking if you say, "How do you do that to yourself?" for something that they think is coming from the outside. My personal preference is to avoid those kinds of presuppositions.

Question: How would you turn *"accident"* into a process? Answer: Try, "What happened accidentally?" Accident is actually a little bit tricky. You accidentally do something or something accidentally occurs. "Accidentally" is actually an adverb, not a verb. But in that case it is still being used as a thing, so you want to break it down. First you will want to recover the deletions by asking, "What happened accidentally?" "Did you slip accidentally?" "Did you crash accidentally?" "Did you cut your finger accidentally?" Then you can ask, "How, specifically, was it accidental?"

Now remember, nominalizations aren't all bad. Nominalizations streamline your communication. If you acted as that department of cartography that I was talking about, and made your map that explicit, it would take you a long time to get anything communicated. In fact, sometimes in asking meta model questions you are just going to gather a lot of information about stuff that isn't important. Then you've got a *meta muddle.* I could go on and on finding out about specifics of this person's early childhood experiences and how they are broken and things that I don't need to know in order to help him change, and I could challenge a lot of nominalizations and find a lot of deletions, but they are not going to help me out that much. I am going to present, later, a way to assist you in knowing when to ask questions and what kinds of questions to ask.

D. Unspecified Verbs

Unspecified verb: Now, an unspecified verb is what you get, a lot of times, when you turn your nominalization back in to the verb form. If a person told me there was a lot of tension in the room, then what I would do would be to put "tension" back into its verb form. "Who is tensing up about what?" Now, if a person just says that he is tense, or that he is feeling very tense, he is using another form of deletion. The essential thing about an unspecified verb is that you want to ask, "*how?*" So, if somebody says, "I know that you are thinking this," you ask, "Well how, specifically, do you know?" You want to find out the rest of the pieces there. If somebody says, "Well, I just went and did this," you ask, "How, specifically, did you do it?" "Did," and "know," and words like that are verbs that are typically unspecified. So, *what you want to do is to recover the adverbs.* How, when, where did you do this, and stuff like that. And recover all those missing pieces. You ask *"How, specifically?"*

Can some people give me examples of unspecified verbs? "Give, how specifically?" you may ask. What about, "I think," "I just know it." Those are unspecified verbs because how, specifically, you *think* and the way you *know* are through your senses. You either talk to yourself about it, make a picture, or get a feeling about it. So, challenging that verb is also going to help you gather information of how people are processing information and how they are thinking. Examples: Wonder, perceive, believe, feel. "Feel" is a good example. "I felt you." "I touched you." "I kissed you." "I caressed you." If I say, "I felt something," that could be referring to any number of sensations, any number of feelings. Those other words got somewhat more specific. If you touch me, I felt your touch. "Touch" is slightly more specified as to what is going on. So is "scratch" and so is "kiss." In fact, "kiss" is the most specified of all those, in its verbal form, because as a predicate, it implies the action, someone kissing someone. It specifies two lips touching.

These first patterns I've just presented I am going to categorize in terms of what we call *information gathering.* These are the most important and basic patterns.

Now, there are other patterns, somewhat easier to observe and challenge and are in a different class, called *limits* to a person's model. These are the kinds of words that you find when people are describing limitations in their behavior or how far they can and cannot go behaviorally.

E. Modal Operators

Modal operators: These are your "cans" and "can'ts:" I *can* do this. I *can't* do this. I *will* do this. I *won't* do this, *must* or *mustn't*, *necessary*, not *necessary*, and these essentially can be condensed into two categories: We have *modal operators of possibility:* It would be *impossible* to change right now, or I just *can't* tell my mother, blah, blah. I *can't* tell my employees this. You are actually saying that something is or isn't *possible.* So we have things like CAN, CAN'T, POSSIBLE, IMPOSSIBLE.

Then you have what you call *modal operators of necessity.* These are "should" and "shouldn't," "have to," "must," it is *important* that I do this. It is *necessary* that I do that.

If a person says, "I *can't* do something," you want to say, "What stops you?" You will be able to get a lot of information about the kinds of things or constraints that they have. So you have, *"What stops you?"*

The response that you offer when a person uses a modal operator of necessity and says, "must," "mustn't," or "should," or "shouldn't," is, "What would happen if you did or didn't?". Sometimes a person doesn't want to do something because he is afraid some catastrophic event would occur if they would go ahead and go through with it. So, *"What would happen?"*

Now, I've been calling these response challenges, but they are not really challenges. They are responses designed to gather higher quality information. When somebody says, "Gosh, it would be really good to do this and I can do this." One of the things that you want to know is, how will they know if they are going to be able to get it accomplished. So you would ask, "What would happen if you could do it?" or, "What is going to happen when you do do it?" so that you can get information about the desired state. Determine what you are going for. What is the desired state or outcome?

F. Presuppositions

Presuppositions: where you already presuppose a thing is happening. If I say, in hypnosis, "Are you going to *go into a trance now* or in five minutes from *now?*" You are presupposing that it is going to happen. The question is just when. You presuppose that the action will occur. So, I say, "What are you going to tell me next week about how much you have changed?" By putting your attention on what you are going to tell me, I am presupposing that *you are going to change.*

If I say, "Did Bill see the cat that is on this table?" What I am asking is, did Bill see it or not, and I am presupposing that there is a cat on this table. Sometimes, people will say something like,

"I would really be able to be happy if only so and so would stop making my life so painful." "If only he'd stop doing this." You are already presupposing that he is. So what you want to say is, "How do you know?" How do you know that this is occurring? How do you know that this is really going to happen? So this question is going to be, *"How do you know?"*

Since you all understand so well, already, I'll just move on. If you want to make a presupposition, all you have to do is start your sentence with "since," and whatever you say after that will have to include some presupposition.

G. Cause-Effect

Cause-effect is actually a form of presupposition, because you are presupposing that something is going to cause something else. My explanation will make you all comfortable that you understand. If I say that Mary causes me a lot of pain, or trouble, or makes me feel bad, or her looking at me like that makes me feel uncomfortable, I am presupposing that there is some connection between those two. This is an example of presupposition, because it presupposes a cause and effect relationship. When you think about it, these are the ways that we essentially have of making sense of our environment. All of our experiences are modeled in terms of cause-effect—that something is going to happen and something will result. In fact, you make extensive use of this pattern in hypnosis with post-hypnotic suggestion. "When I snap my finger *you will all wake up, vibrantly aware and alert. "* Something like that. The thing is that any cause-effect relationship can be valid. If I do snap my fingers and it does make you *vibrant, alive, awake, alert,* and *energetic,* then there is a cause and an effect.

But one of the things that you need to do, if you hear people saying, "She causes me so much pain," and stuff like that, is to ask, "How specifically?" "How do you know *she* does this?" and, "How, specifically, does this happen?" So, you are not just challenging the connection. You want to find out how that connection is there, how it is made. So, this is another one of those "how" questions. How do you know? And *how, specifically, does X cause Y?*

H. Universal Quantifiers

Universal quantifiers: This is one that *everybody* should know. Universal quantifiers are things like "all," "every," "never," and "always," where you are talking about something that may have happened a couple of times and you are generalizing it to all cases. People *always* go away learning so much from my seminars. By the way, all of you probably have begun to realize that there are overlaps in meta model patterns. In other words, universal quantifiers can be considered a form of deletion. Cause-effect is a form of deletion, because I am deleting how the connection is made. So that, actually, a lot of these categories overlap and include another category in them. They are actually interconnected closely.

The challenge to a universal quantifier can be made through exaggeration. You can exaggerate it and say, "It's *always* happened? Or, "You've *never, never* done this?" "Can you think of one instance where she has, or hasn't?" Or something like that where you are going to try and find counterexamples: where you want to exaggerate it into absurdity. If someone says, "She has never cared for me," you say, *"Never, ever?"* "How do you know that?"

"How do you know?" is going to be one of the real important questions for gathering information, especially when you are dealing with people's models of the world, because you will want to know how they make their maps and how they gather information.

1. The Importance of Sensory Experience

By the way, when John and Richard first invented this, they didn't know about accessing cues, so please feel free to use the information that you have available through your other sensory channels. You don't have to hear words for everything. For instance, if I ask someone, "Well, how do you know that?" and they look down and left and say, "Well, I just know it," they have given you the answer. They specifically tell you with their body. So, please use the non-verbal information. These questions are just to help gather information. You don't have to get a verbal answer to get the answer to your question.

For example, if a person looks down and right and says, "I am really confused," you don't have to say, "And how do you know you are confused?" because he is showing you. If a person looks up and left and says, "I am really confused," he is showing you how he is confused. Sometimes people will just tune in to the auditory external verbal stuff and lose a lot of other really important information that is readily available to them. Just keep all of your channels open. The whole concept of secret therapy is based on this. As they think of their problems, clients are giving you enough information with their facial gestures and tonality, so that you don't need to know in words what is going on. You can anchor the 4-tuple you see and hear, and then you can either collapse the anchor or reframe parts, or you can make a label for it. Since words are just anchors, you can create an arbitrary verbal anchor for the experience. If a client says, "You know, I have this real problem," say, "We can call that problem 'blue.' Think of what it's like when you are 'bluing.'" You actually make a label for it. What is important to you is that you know the other person has the map, that he has the representation for the experience or behavior to which you are referring. So, you can *use* the process of nominalization. You can use "blue" as a nominalization for the whole experience and as a resource, because it is an anchor as long as you can see the 4-tuple in his face and other analogues. If you say, "Think of yellow," and he raises eyes up-left, takes a breath and gestures with his left hand—then when you say, "yellow," again and he does the same things, you know he's got that representation anchored to the word "yellow."

2. The Importance of Rapport

Again, you want to temper the meta model questions with rapport. The first seminar I had with John was a linguistics class of about 150 people. John taught the meta model method in an hour or two and had everybody go out and practice it. The next week, when everybody came back to class, about 50 percent of the students claimed that they had lost all their friends, alienated their parents, offended their teachers, and so on. They had become *meta meddlers!* If you go out and ask, "How specifically do you know that you love me?" in a poor tonality, your lover may not respond the way you want. You have to have finesse and sensitivity. You can't question everything. Can you?

I. Lost Performatives

Lost performatives are similar to comparatives in that they are judgments and evaluations except that they don't always involve a comparison. Lost performatives are things such as, "that's *crazy*," "it's *bad*," "you're *resistant*." There, a person is applying a *judgment*, but is *leaving out* who made the evaluation and what criteria were used to make it. What is "lost" in the lost performative are the person and criteria that "performed" the evaluation that produced the judgment. You can recover the lost performative by asking, "Who says it's crazy, bad, or resistant?" and "Crazy according to whom and what criteria?" Some other responses to judgments could be, "Crazy compared to what?" or, "How do you know it is crazy?" or, "Would you be crazy if you did that?" We call that last maneuver *switching referential index*.

J. Mind-Reading

Mind-reading is a pattern that goes along with presupposition. If I said, "I know what you are thinking," or "You don't have to get so upset," I am presupposing that the other person is upset. I am mind-reading them. If you said, "They really hate me," you would be presupposing that you know what is going on in their heads. If I say, "You don't understand what I am saying, do you?" or "You are wondering what I am going to say next," I am mind-reading. Anytime I say, "You are thinking this," or "You are wondering," or "You know this," it is another one of those presuppositions. Saying, "You all know—," is what we call mind-reading, because I am presupposing that I know what is going on in your head. It's also an example of cause-effect, because you are presupposing that some cause is having an effect on somebody else. If I said that you are causing me to feel bad, then that would be an instance of cause-effect. I could mind-read and use cause-effect. I could say, "My talking slowly causes relaxation." Then, I am still using cause-effect, but I am presupposing that it has the same effect on you that it would on me. This can be good information. When somebody is mind-reading you, or mind-reading somebody else, you can probably guess that they would respond with the same reaction that they are hallucinating in the other person.

K. Complex Equivalence

Complex equivalence is essentially finding the 4-tuple a person has for a particular word or generalization. When a person says, "She is not looking at me, she is not paying attention," he is saying that to be paying attention to him you have to be looking at him. Or, "She doesn't love me. She never tells me about her feelings." For that person, love is telling the other person about feelings. Or, "She never touches me," or, "She is never on time, she doesn't love me," or, "It hurts so bad it must be love." When someone makes two experiences equivalent, for example, "Being touched means love," you can challenge him by saying, "Have you ever known you were loved even though you weren't being touched?" Challenge the connection.

Another thing that you can do is use that how-do-you-know question. To be effective with the woman who was overweight I had to find out what would constitute, in her mind, effective therapy. In other words, what is the person's complex equivalence for what I should be doing to help them? "What do I need to do? What is equivalent to your changing?" One of the first things you do in the induction of hypnosis is to ask, "How would you know if you were in a trance?" "What is your equivalence, in terms of what you would feel, hear, or see, for what a trance state is?" Do the same thing for "change." "What would you need to see, hear, or feel to make the change that you want to?" You want to find out what set of experiences is going to mean "change," is going to mean "trance," or whatever it is you are gathering information about. In some cases, you will want to challenge it, depending on how you perceive what is going on with the person, and depending upon the intervention that you want to make.

From audience: "Give some examples of *complex equivalence*." Answer: "If you ask that question, you don't understand something." I am saying that your asking that question *means* that you don't understand something. That may be very valid (again, this is not necessarily invalid). If I say, "You are nodding your head, you must have gotten something out of my answer," I may be accurate. I am saying that your nodding your head means that *you do understand*, or that *you have gotten something out of it*. Another one is: If they are fidgeting, they are nervous. So that means, fidgeting means nervousness. There may be some overlap with mind-reading.

But if I am talking about change and I say, "I can challenge nominalizations, I have changed," then I am not mind-reading, but I am saying that because I can do this, that *means* I have changed.

That reminds me of a story I heard John Grinder tell. A psychology professor he had in college was lecturing about the limitations of attention, saying, "You can only pay attention about forty-five minutes or so." This teacher talked on non-stop for two and a half hours on how attention span was only 45 minutes (laughter). So what I was thinking was that we would give ourselves a break and give ourselves a break. Then what I would like to do is to have you all form groups of fours and do some exercises where you will learn to identify these patterns.

Now what I am going to have you do in the exercise is this: Each of you pick one of these patterns, generate a bunch of them, and have the other people identify which one you are doing, and how many you are doing with each other. I want you to each practice generating these as well as challenging them.

Let's take a five minute break and be back in ten minutes (laughter). Will everybody who has studied meta model before raise your hand. What I would like to do is to have you continue raising your hands until they become cataleptic (laughter). Actually, I would like to have at least one of these people in your groups. I would like to have at least one person who knows it very well. Let's go *do it!*

(After exercise) : John was doing a workshop for lawyers the other day, and my father, who is a patent attorney, was pointing out that there is a trick that a lot of lawyers do called "double questions." I say to the person on the box, "Well, you did 'x' and then you went to their house, didn't you?" The person may very well have gone to their house but I am tacking and you did "X" on the same question. Then the lawyer says, "Just answer yes or no," or, "Just answer the question now." If the person says, "No, I didn't," he acts like that person is being incongruent or lying, because there was this incongruent representation. Part of the statement was accurate. That is a very interesting sort of pattern. I don't think normal people use it that much.

III. Comments on the Use of the Meta Model

What I want to do is find out if anyone found out anything interesting. I would like to point out a couple of things: (1) I would like to explain the difference between mind-reading and lost performatives. When a person says, "You are tired," he is mind-reading. "You are tired," means that I am reading into them an internal state. A lost performative is something that is a judgment. If I say, "You are bad," "You are nasty," or "You are fraudulent and unprofessional," I am not describing an internal state, I am passing a judgment.

If I say, "You are confused," I am not making a judgment as much as I am trying to identify your internal state. If I tell you that you are bad, then I am putting a judgment on you. If I say that you are tired, that is a state that you can go into. If I say that you are nasty then I'm evaluating you. A lot of mind-reading statements may have judgmental connotations. But lost performatives are generally a statement of a judgment as if it were a property of reality as opposed to a description of what is going on inside the other person.

(2) Another thing is that words like "I am *patient*," "You are *confused*," "I feel *curious*," are adverbs, a class of predicates—you know adjectives and adverbs, like saying, "The grass is green." It is not like saying, "The grass is a chair." If it were really a nominalization it would fit into the same class. In the meta model you break down adjectives and adverbs like you would an unspecified verb. That is, "how specifically?"

(3) Sometimes modal operators of necessity can have a lot of bad anchors associated with them, for example, "I *should* do this, "I *should* do that." If you change those to modal operators of possibility, "I *can* do this, I *can* do that,"—it makes a big difference in the way the client feels, or the way that he thinks about it. Try

saying to your clients, "I am wondering if you would substitute the word 'can' or 'want' for 'should' in the statement you just made?" Both words share the same classification, that is they are both modal operators, but have different connotations.

(4) Complex equivalence patterns can be a positive thing, but they may also cause limitations. In a sense, it involves a limitation. I draw a direct equivalence. The person who is auditory listens to another by tilting his head to the side so his ear faces the person. The visual person says, "He is not paying attention, he is not looking at me." So, for the visual person, paying attention is the equivalent of looking. For that person "attention" is an unnecessarily limited set of experiences. Actually, "complex equivalence" could more aptly be renamed "simplistic equivalence."

(5) As an organizing principle: You've got to find a person's complex equivalence for a desired state. Ask, "How are you going to know that you've achieved your outcome?" "What specifically will be going on when you achieve your goal?" That is a positive use of it. That is important. The meta model doesn't imply that the patterns we've been talking about are bad. I use nominalizations a lot. John and Richard use nominalizations. Words are labels and labeling is in itself neither good, nor bad. The thing that is important is to know what responses they are eliciting.

(6) You are mind-reading when you leave out the complex equivalence you used to make the computation about the person's internal experience. Using accessing cues is a way to mind-read without leaving out that computation. You learn accessing cues to read people's minds more effectively.

(7) In regard to handling universal quantifiers: Find a *counter-example*, "Was there a time when this did not happen?" If they say, "No one has ever liked me," you can provide them with an ongoing counter-example, "How do you know I don't like you?" Something like that. If someone says, "Everybody thinks I am crazy," you say, "I don't think you are crazy." In other words, you can also use yourself as a challenge, or set it up so that you can do that.

(8) Phenomenology is the philosophy of nominalizations.

(9) The meta model is perhaps one of the most profound ways that I know of to put somebody else into a trance. You are forcing them to go into downtime to recover all the deep structure. They have to go inside and do a transderivational search, age regress, and all those other things, to find the reference experience you are asking about. It is one of the fastest ways to put people into an altered state.

Robert Dilts

Appendix 3

Linguistic Presuppositions

Simple Presuppositions

These are syntactic environments in which the existence of some entity is required for the sentence to make sense.

Proper names.

George Smith left the party early. => There exists someone named George Smith.

Pronouns.

Her, him, they. I saw *him* leave. => There exists some male (i.e. him)

Definite Descriptions.

I liked *the woman with the silver earrings.* => There exists a woman with silver earrings.

Generic Noun Phrases.

Noun arguments standing for a whole class. If *wombats* have no trees to climb in, they are sad. => There are wombats.

Some Quantifiers.

All, each, every, some, many, few, none.
If some of the dragons show up, I'm leaving. => There are dragons.

Complex Presuppositions

Cases in which more than the simple existence of an element is presupposed.

Relative Clauses.

Complex noun arguments, with a noun followed by a phrase beginning with *who, which*, or *that*.
Several of the women who had spoken to you left the shop. =>
Several women had spoken to you.

Subordinate Clauses of Time.

Clauses identified by the cue words *before, after, during, as, since, prior, when, while*.
If the judge was home *when I stopped by her house*, she didn't answer her door. => I stopped by the judge's house.

Cleft Sentence.

Sentences beginning with It was/is noun argument.
It was the extra pressure that shattered the window. =>
Something shattered the window.

Pseudo-Cleft Sentences.

Identified by the form *What* [sentence] *is* [sentence].
What Sharon hopes to do is to become well-liked. => Sharon hopes to do something.

Stressed Sentences.

Voice stress.
If Margaret has talked to THE POLICE, we're finished. =>
Margaret has talked to someone.

Complex Adjectives.

New, old, former, present, previous.
If Fredo wears his *new* ring, I'll be blown away. => Fredo has/had an old ring.

Ordinal Numerals.

First, second, third, fourth, another.
If you can find a *third* clue in this letter, I'll make you a mosquito pie. => There are two clues already found.

Comparatives.

-er, more, less.
If you know *better* riders than Sue does, tell me who they are. => Sue knows [at least] one rider.

Comparative As.

As x as...
If her daughter is as funny as her husband is, we'll all enjoy ourselves. => Her husband is funny.

Repetitive Cue Words.

Too, also, whether, again, back
If she tells me that *again*, I'll kiss her. => She has told me that before.

Repetitive Verbs and Adverbs.

Verbs and adverbs beginning with *re-*, e.g., *repeatedly, return, restore, retell, replace, renew.*
If he *re*turns before I leave, I want to talk to him. => He has been here before.

Qualifiers.

Only, even, except, just.
Only Amy saw the bank robbers. => Amy saw the bank robbers.

Change-of-Place Verbs.

Come, go, leave, arrive, depart, enter.
If Sam has *left* home, he is lost. => Sam has been at home.

Change-of-Time Verbs and Adverbs.

Begin, end, stop, start, continue, proceed, already, yet, still, anymore.
My bet is that Harry will *continue* to smile. => Harry has been smiling.

Change-of-State Verbs.

Change, transform, turn into, become.
If Mae *turns into* a hippie, I'll be surprised. => Mae is not now a hippie.

Factive Verbs and Adjectives.

Odd, aware, know, realize, regret.
It is *odd* that she called Maxine at midnight. => She called Maxine at midnight.

Commentary Adjectives and Adverbs.

Lucky, fortunate, far out, out of sight, groovy, bitchin, ... innocently, happily, necessarily.
It's *far out* that you understand your dog's feelings. => You understand your dog's feelings.

Counterfactual Conditional Clauses.

Verbs having subjunctive tense.
If you had listened to me and your father, you wouldn't be in the wonderful position you're in now. => You didn't listen to me and your father.

Contrary-to-Expectation.

Should.
If you should [happen to] decide you want to talk to me, I'll be hanging out in the city dump. => I don't expect that you want to talk to me.

strictions.

fessor gets *pregnant*, I'll be disappointed. => My pro-
a woman.

Questions.

Who ate the tapes? => Someone ate the tapes.
I want to know who ate the tapes. => Someone ate the tapes.

Negative Questions.

Didn't you want to talk to me? => I thought you wanted to talk
to me.

Rhetorical Questions.

Who cares about whether you show up or not? => Nobody cares
whether you show up or not.

Spurious Not.

I wonder if you're *not* being a little unfair. => I think you're
being unfair.

Appendix 4

Submodalities

The whole meta-model describes a few of the most useful submodality distinctions of language. We placed submodalities after the meta-model to match the practical sequence. We use the meta-model to explore submodalities.

After you acquire Richard's skills, you will be able to elicit submodalities covertly in casual conversation. Till then you may want to use what I do.

People usually have strong opinions about movies and television programs. I want to make some documentaries and film some scripts. People tell me, in great detail, how to do it properly.

They describe the camera angles, sound quality, etc., necessary to be convincing or dreamlike. Then we may talk about what we would do if available technology did not limit us in any way. We could create any experience.

That may lead us to realize that we all do that all the time all by ourselves.

SUB-MODALITIES

VISUAL	AUDITORY	KINESTHETIC
BRIGHTNESS	VOLUME	INTENSITY
(dim-bright)	(loud-soft)	(**strong**-weak)
SIZE	TONE	AREA
(large-small)	(bass-treble)	(large-small)
COLOR	PITCH	TEXTURE
(black & white-color)	(high-low)	(rough-smooth)
MOVEMENT	TEMPO	DURATION
(fast-slow-still)	(fast-slow)	(constant-intermittent)
DISTANCE	DISTANCE	TEMPERATURE
(near-far)	(close-far)	(hot-cold)
FOCUS	RHYTHM	WEIGHT
(clear-fuzzy)		(**heavy**-light)
LOCATION	LOCATION	LOCATION
DEPTH		
(3D-flat)		

META-MODALITIES

ASSOCIATED-DISSOCIATED	WORDS-TONES	EMOTIONAL-TACTILE
INTERNAL-EXTERNAL	INTERNAL-EXTERNAL	INTERNAL-EXTERNAL

Appendix 5

Reframing

Reframing Outline

(1) *Set up yes/no signals with the unconscious.*

(2) *Identify a pattern of behavior to be changed.* Ask her unconscious to select some behavior, X, that *it* doesn't like. Ask it to pick something that it thinks is of utmost and vital importance to her well-being. Have it give you a "yes" signal when it has identified one.

(3) *Separate positive function from behavior.*

    (a) Ask her unconscious mind to turn the yes/no signals over to the part of her that makes her do X. Either ask that part to give you a "yes" signal, or a "yes" and a "no" signal simultaneously, when that has occurred.

    (b) Ask, "Are you willing to allow her conscious mind to know what is of value that occurs when she does X?" If "yes," say, "Go ahead and let her know, and when you've done that, give me a 'yes' signal." If "no," proceed.

(4) *Create new alternatives.*

    (a) Ask that part if it would be willing to go into the person's creative resources and get new ways to accomplish this

positive function other than X. (The part is under no obliga-
tion to accept or use these choices, only to find them.)

(b) When you get a "yes," tell it to go ahead, and give you a
"yes" signal when it has ten new choices.

(5) *Evaluate new alternatives.*

(a) Ask that part to evaluate each new choice in terms of
whether unconsciously it believes the choice is at least as
immediate, effective and available as X. Each time the
part identifies one that it believes *is*, have it give you a
"yes" signal.

(b) If you get less than three, recycle to step (4) and get more
choices.

(6) *Select one alternative.*

(a) Ask the part to select the new way it considers the most
satisfying and available in achieving the positive function,
and to give you a "yes" signal when it has selected.

(b) Ask the unconscious part if it would be responsible for
using this new choice for three weeks to evaluate its
effectiveness.

(7) *Future-Pace.* Ask her unconscious to go into a fantasy of trying out the new behaviors in the appropriate context. Have
her unconscious notify you either "yes" it's working, or "no" it
isn't. If there is any way in which the new choice doesn't work
or has harmful side effects, recycle to step (4) and create new
choices.

Appendix 6

Toning Up Your Voice

In this book, Richard has put more emphasis than ever before on developing our voices as a powerful tool. In hypnosis people become more sensitive and responsive to intonation. Regression exaggerates this further. Before birth, our mother's voice resounds through us. Our first knowledge of the outside world comes through sound.

Unfortunately, working voice instruction into the text presents difficulties of both grace and practicality. Putting this material in an appendix makes it less awkward and more convenient for you. There remains the challenge of working, yourself, on your own voice. As Richard remarks, today we have recorders. Use one.

If you can find competent voice coaches, use them. Finding anyone competent at anything provides another challenge. More, even the earliest training in NLP led to greater demands and more stringent definitions of competence. A person who is a good voice coach for you can, in your first session, elicit an attractive and useful change in your voice and tell you how to sustain it. If not, move on. Without competent face-to-face instruction, you will probably get better results working with yourself, a tape recorder, and friends.

Our voice comes from what we do inside our bodies. The visible way we use our bodies may relate to psychic alignment, balance, and attitude. Some deep patterns of voice may relate to integrity. Making changes in our voice requires us to change patterns of relaxation and tension inside our bodies. That literally changes the way we feel inside. This often relates to issues of identity. No wonder so many of us have found a standing challenge in our own voices. These ideas may suggest new values in that challenge.

Many books have been written about voice control. I have yet to find one using NLP. You may use these necessarily brief notes as a base for your own.

We can control our voice with our lips, jaw, tongue, neck, throat, chest, and diaphragm. We have a lot more equipment than we need. Ventriloquists learn to speak with no visible use of their lips or jaw.

Start a systematic and silly inventory of all these variables. Record yourself running through the full range of each in various combinations with the others. Take notes. Record yourself making the goofiest sounds you can. Make faces. Get videotapes of Rich Little, Robin Williams, Whoopi Goldberg, Lily Tomlin, etc. in solo performance. Play them and play with them. If we receive a demand for it, we may do a book about voice development.

My own voice changes dramatically and attractively when I open my mouth and move my tongue forward, say a half inch each. This pulls the soft palate away from the sinuses, allowing more resonance. Pushing or pursing the lips forward can also make for more resonance in the mouth itself. So stick out your lips, stick out your jaw, and stick out your tongue.

Fortunately, many people have pleasant experiences which involve having their lips forward, their jaws open, their tongues out, and all of them mobile. If you have any of those, you may enjoy using a particularly good one as an anchor for your voice. Here in Salt Lake City, we pretend to lick an ice cream cone.

Glossary of NLP Terms

Accessing Cues Subtle behaviors that will both help to trigger and indicate which representational system a person is using to think with. Typical types of accessing cues include eye movements, voice tone and tempo, body posture, gestures, and breathing patterns.

Anchoring The process of associating an internal response with some external trigger (similar to classical conditioning) so that the response may be quickly, and sometimes covertly, reaccessed.

Auditory Relating to hearing or the sense of hearing.

Behavior The specific physical actions and reactions through which we interact with the people and environment around us.

Behavioral Flexibility The ability to vary one's own behavior in order to elicit or secure a response from another person.

Beliefs Closely held generalizations about (1) cause, (2) meaning, and (3) boundaries in (a) the world around us, (b) our behavior, (c) our capabilities, and (d) our identities. Beliefs function at a different level than concrete reality and serve to guide and interpret our perceptions of reality, often by connecting them to our criteria or value systems. Beliefs are notoriously difficult to change through typical rules of logic or rational thinking.

Calibration The process of learning to read another person's unconscious, non-verbal responses in an ongoing interaction by pairing observable behavioral cues with a specific internal response.

Calibrated Loop Unconscious pattern of communication in which behavioral cues of one person trigger specific responses from another person in an ongoing interaction.

Capability Mastery over an entire class of behavior—knowing how to do something. Capabilities come from the development of a mental map that allows us to select and organize groups of individual behaviors. In NLP these mental maps take the form of cognitive strategies and metaprograms.

Chunking Organizing or breaking down some experience into bigger or smaller pieces. Chunking up involves moving to a larger, more abstract level of information. Chunking down involves moving to a more specific and concrete level of information. Chunking laterally involves finding other examples at the same level of information.

Congruence When all of a person's internal beliefs, strategies, and behaviors are fully in agreement and oriented toward securing a desired outcome.

Context The framework surrounding a particular event. This framework will often determine how a particular experience or event is interpreted.

Criteria The values or standards a person uses to make decisions and judgments.

Deep Structure The sensory maps (both conscious and unconscious) that people use to organize and guide their behavior.

Environment The external context in which our behavior takes place. Our environment is that which we perceive as being "outside" of us. It is not part of our behavior but is rather something we must react to.

Four Tuple (or 4-tuple) A shorthand method used to notate the structure of any particular experience. The concept of the four tuple maintains that any experience must be composed of some combination of the four primary representational classes—<A,V,K,O>—where A = auditory, V = visual, K = kinesthetic, and O = olfactory/gustatory.

Future Pacing The process of mentally rehearsing oneself through some future situation in order to help ensure that the desired behavior will occur naturally and automatically.

Gustatory Relating to taste or the sense of taste.

Identity Our sense of who we are. Our sense of identity organizes our beliefs, capabilities, and behaviors into a single system.

Installation The process of facilitating the acquisition of a new strategy or behavior. A new strategy may be installed through some combination of anchoring, accessing cues, metaphor, and future pacing.

Kinesthetic Relating to body sensations. In NLP the term kinesthetic is used to encompass all kinds of feelings including tactile, visceral, and emotional.

Logical Levels An internal hierarchy in which each level is progressively more psychologically encompassing and impactful. In order of importance (from high to low) these levels include (1) identity, (2) beliefs, (3) capabilities, (4) behavior, and (5) environment.

Meta Model A model developed by John Grinder and Richard Bandler that identifies categories of language patterns that can be problematic or ambiguous.

Meta Program A level of mental programming that determines how we sort, orient to, and chunk our experiences. Our meta programs are more abstract than our specific strategies for thinking and define our general approach to a particular issue rather than the details of our thinking process.

Metaphor The process of thinking about one situation or phenomenon as something else, i.e., stories, parables, and analogies.

Modeling The process of observing and mapping the successful behaviors of other people.

Neuro-Linguistic Programming (NLP) A behavioral model and set of explicit skills and techniques founded by John Grinder and Richard Bandler in 1975. Defined as the study of the structure of subjective experience. NLP studies the patterns or "programming" created by the interaction among the brain (neuro), language (linguistic), and the body that produce both effective and ineffective behavior. The skills and techniques were derived by observing the patterns of excellence in experts from diverse fields of professional communication, including psychotherapy, business, hypnosis, law, and education.

Olfactory Relating to smell or the sense of smell.

Outcomes Goals or desired states that a person or organization aspires to achieve.

Pacing A method used by communicators to quickly establish rapport by matching certain aspects of their behavior to those of the person with whom they are communicating—a matching or mirroring of behavior.

Parts A metaphorical way of talking about independent programs and strategies of behavior. Programs or "parts" will often develop a persona that becomes one of their identifying features.

Position A particular perspective or point of view. In NLP there are three basic positions one can take in perceiving a particular experience. First position involves experiencing something through our own eyes associated in a first person point of view. Second position involves experiencing something as if we were in another person's shoes. Third position involves standing back and perceiving the relationship between ourselves and others from a dissociated perspective.

Predicates Process words (like verbs, adverbs, and adjectives) that a person selects to describe a subject. Predicates are used in NLP to identify which representational system a person is using to process information.

Quotes A pattern in which a message that you want to deliver can be embedded in quotations, as if someone else had stated the message.

Rapport The establishment of trust, harmony, and cooperation in a relationship.

Reframing A process used in NLP through which a problematic behavior is separated from the positive intention of the internal program or "part" that is responsible for the behavior. New choices of behavior are established by having the part responsible for the old behavior take responsibility for implementing other behaviors that satisfy the same positive intention but don't have the problematic byproducts.

Representational Systems The five senses: seeing, hearing, touching (feeling), smelling, and tasting.

Representational System Primacy Where an individual systematically uses one sense over the others to process and organize his or her experience. Primary representational system will determine many personality traits as well as learning capabilities.

Secondary Gain Where some seemingly negative or problematic behavior actually carries out some positive function at some other level. For example, smoking may help a person to relax or help them fit a particular self-image.

State The total ongoing mental and physical conditions from which a person is acting.

Strategy A set of explicit mental and behavioral steps used to achieve a specific outcome. In NLP, the most important aspect of a strategy is the representational systems used to carry out the specific steps.

Sub-Modalities The special sensory qualities perceived by each of the senses. For example, visual sub-modalities include color, shape, movement, brightness, depth, etc., auditory sub-modalities include volume, pitch, tempo, etc., and kinesthetic sub-modalities include pressure, temperature, texture, location, etc.

Surface Structure The words or language used to describe or stand for the actual primary sensory representations stored in the brain.

Synesthesia The process of overlap between representational systems, characterized by phenomena like see-feel circuits, in which a person derives feelings from what he sees, and hear-feel circuits, in which a person gets feelings from what they hear. Any two sensory modalities may be linked together.

T.O.T.E. Developed by Miller, Galanter and Pribram, the term stands for the sequence Test-Operate-Test-Exit, which describes the basic feedback loop used to guide all behavior.

Transderivational Search The process of searching back through one's stored memories and mental representations to find the reference experience from which a current behavior or response was derived.

Translating The process of rephrasing words from one type of representational system predicates to another.

Utilization A technique in which a specific strategy sequence or pattern of behavior is paced or matched in order to influence another's response.

Visual Relating to sight or the sense of sight.

Well-Formedness Conditions The set of conditions something must satisfy in order to produce an effective and ecological outcome. In NLP a particular goal is well-formed if it can be: (1) stated in positive terms, (2) defined and evaluated according to sensory based evidence, (3) initiated and maintained by the person who desires the goal, (4) made to preserve the positive byproducts of the present state, and (5) appropriately contextualized to fit the external ecology.

The Society of
Neuro-Linguistic Programming™

Established in 1978, the Society of Neuro-Linguistic Programming™ is a worldwide organization set up for the purpose of exerting quality control over those training programs and services claiming to represent the model of Neuro-Linguistic Programming™ (NLP). The seal above indicates Society Certification and is usually advertised by Society approved institutes and centers. We highly recommend that you exercise caution as you apply the techniques and skills of NLP. We also urge you to attend only those seminars, workshops and training programs that been officially designed and certified by The Society of Neuro-Linguistic Programming™. Any training programs that have been approved and endorsed by The Society of Neuro-Linguistic Programming™ will display a copy of the registered certification mark(s) of the Society of Neuro-Linguistic Programming™. The Society of Neuro-Linguistic Programming™ is set up for the purpose of exerting quality control over those training programs, services and materials claiming to represent the model of Neuro-Linguistic Programming™.

As a protection for you and for those around you, The Society of NLP™ requires participants to sign licensing agreements which guarantees that those certified and licensed in this technology will use it with the highest integrity. It is also a way to insure that all the trainings you attend are of the highest quality and that your trainers are updated and current with the constant evolution of the field of Neuro-Linguistic Programming™ and Design Human Engineering™.

There are four levels of certification and licensing granted by The Society of Neuro-Linguistic Programming™: Practitioner, Master Practitioner, Trainer and Master Trainer. All certificates issued by The Society of Neuro-Linguistic Programming™, the Society seal, and Richard Bandler's signature in penned ink. Trainers may train Practitioners and Master Practitioners who then may get certified and licensed by Richard Bandler and The Society of Neuro-Linguistic Programming™. Master Trainer is a level recognized because of special circumstances and contributions. This level is reserved and can only be granted by Richard Bandler and The Society of Neuro-Linguistic Programming™. Master Trainers may not certify Trainers except under special written permission of Dr. Bandler.

Design Human Engineering™ (DHE) may only be trained by Trainers of DHE. This level of certification is granted only by Richard Bandler and The Society of Neuro-Linguistic Programming™. Their certificate will specifically state "Trainer of Design Human Engineering™" with the Society Seal and Richard Bandler's signature.

To be sure you are purchasing Pure NLP products and/or services, please call the Society of Neuro-Linguistic Programming™. We are most interested in protecting the technology's integrity. All certifications and licensing carry a two (2) year expiration date, the Society Seal, and Richard Bandler's signature. You have the right to ask anyone advertising NLP services to show you their license and/or certification. An inability to produce this document may one of two possibilities: either the person and/or organization is defrauding the public, or they have been defrauded themselves by another organization purporting to be a certifying organization. Under either condition, please notify The Society of Neuro-Linguistic Programming™ so that we may take steps to rectify the situation.

Each license and/or certification has a two year expiration date. This is because the technology is constantly evolving and Dr. Bandler is continuing his development contributions to human evolution. The Society expects that those who hold certification continually update their skills and renew their certifications and/or licenses. Renewal is not automatic and is easy. Do not accept certifications and/or licenses without expiration dates. If you have benefited from Richard's contributions in the form of the technologies he has developed, we appreciate it when you help us to point out the charlatans who are out there misinforming the public. This is more of a moral issue than anything else. Richard and the Society are interested in people doing the right things and becoming very prosperous in all areas of their lives. There is an unlimited amount of opportunity for everyone. There is no need to steal.

If you are certified at any level of Design Human Engineering™, you must obtain express written permission for each usage of the term or symbol (DHE™) from Richard Bandler. This can be obtained by contacting the First Institute of NLP™ and DHE™ at (415) 955-0541 or 44 Montgomery St., 5th floor, San Francisco, Ca. 94104. Each use of the term Design Human Engineering™ must be earmarked with a (™) as well as a symbol that refers to the phrase "Design Human Engineering™ and DHE™ is used with express written permission of Richard Bandler."

ONLY RICHARD BANDLER, PERSONALLY, MAY TRAIN TRAINERS OF NLP™, except under express written permission from Richard Bandler.

Should you be a member of the Society of Neuro-Linguistic Programming™ and have not complied with the above requirements, we wish to make you aware that you may grandfather your trainees for a limited time.

The Society publishes its directory of members in good standing and is happy to provide referrals upon request and encourages participation in this opportunity to make a difference for everyone.